Woman OF Strength

LIVING THE BEST LIFE POSSIBLE
FOR god IN THIS BROKEN WORLD

Alice Mathews

Our Daily Bread
Publishing™

Requests for permission to quote from this book should be directed to: Permissions Department, Our Daily Bread Publishing, PO Box 3566, Grand Rapids, MI 49501, or contact us by email at permissionsdept@odb.org.

Scripture quotations, unless otherwise indicated, are taken from the Holy Bible, New International Version®, NIV®. Copyright © 1973, 1978, 1984, 2011 by Biblica, Inc.™ Used by permission of Zondervan. All rights reserved worldwide. www.zondervan.com.
  Scripture quotations marked KJV are from the King James Version.
  Scripture quotations marked NKJV are from the New King James Version®. Copyright © 1982 by Thomas Nelson. Used by permission. All rights reserved.
  Scripture quotations marked NLT are taken from the Holy Bible, New Living Translation, copyright ©1996, 2004, 2015 by Tyndale House Foundation. Used by permission of Tyndale House Publishers, Inc., Carol Stream, Illinois 60188. All rights reserved.
  Scripture quotations marked NRSV are from New Revised Standard Version Bible, copyright © 1989 National Council of the Churches of Christ in the United States of America. Used by permission. All rights reserved.

Interior design by Jessica Ess, Hillspring Books

Library of Congress Cataloging-in-Publication Data

Names: Mathews, Alice, 1930- author.
Title: Woman of strength : living the best life possible for God in this broken world / Alice Mathews.
Description: Grand Rapids, MI : Our Daily Bread Publishing, 2020. | Summary: "Through careful translation, practical application, and reflection questions, you will discover what Proverbs 31 reveals about women, about men, and about God himself"-- Provided by publisher.
Identifiers: LCCN 2020014608 | ISBN 9781640700499 (paperback)
Subjects: LCSH: Bible. Proverbs, XXXI, 10-31--Criticism, interpretation, etc.
Classification: LCC BS1465.52 .M365 2020 | DDC 248.8/43--dc23
LC record available at https://lccn.loc.gov/2020014608

Printed in the United States of America
21 22 23 24 25 26 27 / 8 7 6 5 4 3 2

To Dr. Karen Mason,
whose early insights into Proverbs 31 gave me hope

And to Dr. Bruce Waltke,
whose erudition in the Hebrew text confirmed that hope

Contents

1

A Call to Live Your Best Life

When I was very young, my father often read to me just before bedtime. My all-time favorite book was *The Little Engine That Could*. In it, a big and powerful engine had broken down. No other big engine was available. So the Little Engine was given an almost impossible task—to pull that long, heavy line of train cars up over the mountain in time for the children's Christmas. I'm told that long before I could read, I could recite the words on each page and turn the pages at the right moment. I never tired of the Little Engine puffing, "I think I can, I think I can, I think I can," even as it strained to pull that long train.

Recently, I've realized how much my basic attitude toward life has been shaped by the message of that book. Although I consider myself a realist, not just a merry optimist, I tend to approach difficulties as opportunities to be faced and overcome. Over the decades, I've continued to read "little engine" books—books that in some way remind us that we can almost always find a way to address the challenges of life. As a follower of Jesus Christ, I have also read books that, with God's help and approval, give me strength and wisdom to tackle the next problem or to move on to the next challenge, not just from a positive perspective but from a distinctly Christian one. And from time to time, this has posed a challenge of its own.

The challenge is that instead of empowering and equipping me, some Christian books I've read over the decades have felt *dis*empowering and limiting, particularly those written to me as a Christian woman. So what am I to do with such books, ones that seem to constrict my life, to fence me in, to restrict the way in which I am allowed to use my gifts and skills? If I decide to read them, looking for the gospel truth in them to guide my life, what effect do they have on my actions and emotions? If I'm honest, I have to admit I seldom read such books to the end. After reading a chapter or two and feeling deflated about the way the writer has erected fences around a Christian woman's life, I tend to cast the book aside. Such books often quote (or misquote) a few Bible verses to support the fences they want to build around my life, but life is tough enough without adding more obstacles and limitations!

Yet, at the same time, I also want to avoid making errors in my own understanding of biblical principles. That's when I worry about what I've read: *What if those books are right? What if God has in fact erected those fences? Is it possible that I'm called to set aside my gifts or settle for a narrower understanding of God's will and purpose for my life?*

These are significant questions, and I know that I'm not the only Christian woman asking them. Over the years, I've met scores of Christian women struggling with the same questions. Some have gone along with those restrictive teachings and settled for a narrower life. Others have challenged those teachings, fighting for a different understanding of God's Word and what it says about their place in the world. Still others have simply walked away from anything

"Christian."

In my case, I didn't want to settle for a narrow life, nor did I want to walk away from the Christian life. I wanted to challenge those restrictive teachings because I was dissatisfied with what some theologians were proclaiming as "gospel truth" for the acceptable attitudes and behaviors of a Christian woman. Many based their conclusions, at least in part, on the final chapter of the Old Testament book called Proverbs—the infamous Proverbs 31. I listened to their sermons. I read their interpretations. And all the while, something didn't ring true. I couldn't put my finger on the problem, and I worried that perhaps they were right, and I needed to make sure my life conformed to their teachings.

But then a breakthrough came. My daughter Karen, then an Old Testament major in seminary, took a course on Proverbs from noted scholar Bruce Waltke. Bruce was clear: the Proverbs 31 woman was *hayil*—she was a woman of strength. What did that mean? And what, specifically, should that look like for women today? I had so many questions! It was time to take a deep dive into the biblical text.

As I studied the text, what I found was a list of daunting activities this model woman carried out. Years earlier, I had heard a famous teacher of preachers comment that a list is the hardest kind of biblical text to preach. Lists usually consist of items that are only incidentally related. There's some reason why each item is on the list, but a list doesn't necessarily have an obvious flow of thought that enables a preacher to craft a unified sermon. That said, the teacher of preaching went on to note that Proverbs 31:10–31 is a prime example of such a list. Each item pretty much stands alone. The list doesn't begin at one point and then gradually build to a climax. Instead, it simply notes a variety of items in no particular order, making it difficult for a preacher to land a unified point with power at the sermon's end.

That teacher's observations made sense to me because I had listened to a number of sermons preached on Proverbs 31, and that's what I'd heard—a list of points in no particular order. It seemed that preachers could decide on their own what each verse should mean, and then expect me to live up to their ideal for the Proverbs 31 woman.

I'd wince, uncomfortable and unconvinced by what I was hearing. But there it was, in the Bible. I couldn't deny that. Furthermore, my strong commitment to Scripture forced me to grapple with each of the verses in Proverbs 31. I knew that under the inspiration of God the Holy Spirit "*all* Scripture is God-breathed and is useful for teaching, rebuking, correcting and training in righteousness, so that the servant of God may be thoroughly equipped for every good work" (2 Timothy 3:16–17, emphasis added). Proverbs 31:10–31 was part of Scripture. I couldn't ignore it. I also knew it was a piece of the Bible designed to "equip me for every good work." But when I began a deep dive into Proverbs 31, I was surprised again and again by what I discovered. In fact, I identified five surprises that changed the way I now see this much misunderstood and much maligned passage of Scripture. What a difference these five surprises have made! They've tossed in the dustbin the notion that a Christian woman is bound by a narrow and limited life. Instead, they have allowed Proverbs 31 to open wide the possibilities for every woman to live her best life.

Surprise 1: Proverbs 31 is not addressed to women.

When preachers take a congregation through these verses in one of those "list" sermons, more often than not, they make the point that the text is for and about women. Most people don't notice that Proverbs 31 is not addressed to women. But it's true. The chapter contains advice given to King Lemuel by the queen mother, advice designed to equip the king and other rulers to govern wisely.

What did the king need to consider? What could or should he embrace? What should he shun? For example, he's told, "Do not spend your strength on women, your vigor on those who ruin kings" (31:3). That sounds specific and all-inclusive: avoid *all* women. But is this sweeping statement meant to include all women or only a certain kind of woman? Old Testament scholar Bruce Waltke suggests that it could refer to avoiding seductive women outside of marriage (Proverbs 2:16–19, 5:1–23; 6:20–35; 7:1–27). Or it might refer to women in a large harem of concubines (1 Kings 11:11; Esther 2:10–14). In any case, obsession with the wrong kind of women had the power to corrupt a king's ability to rule and to waste his money. We see the truth of that teaching as we watch Solomon's seven hundred wives and three hundred concubines "turn his heart after other gods" (1 Kings 11:3–4).

So King Lemuel is cautioned against linking up with the wrong kind of women, but note that he is not called to lead a celibate life. Instead, the king is introduced to the right kind of woman, a *hayil* woman of strength (Proverbs 31:10). Her worth is beyond the value of the most precious gems. A wise man will opt for the right kind of woman, a *hayil* woman of strength.

Surprise 2: A woman sets the right example for the king.
Proverbs 31 consists of two poems—the first in verses 1–9 and the second in verses 10–31. Some Bible scholars think only the first of the two poems was directed to the king, but the two poems are linked together in such a way that we have to take them together. In addition to the link about the right kind of woman in contrast to those women who "destroy kings,"

King Lemuel is directed to, "Speak up for those who cannot speak for themselves, for the rights of all who are destitute. Speak up and judge fairly; defend the rights of the poor and needy" (31:8–9). Then in verse 20, he learns that a woman of strength will do just that: she will use her resources to help the poor and needy. Thus, a woman in the second poem models the correct values for the king. So when we read Proverbs 31, we do well to begin with verse 1 and understand that all wise people need the kind of advice King Lemuel was given. This is the practical wisdom that keeps people from making foolish decisions. The chapter as a whole is instructive for all of us, women and men, helping us discover what makes for a truly wise person.

Surprise 3: The book of Proverbs begins and ends with a strong and wise woman.

Proverbs is a collection of wise sayings, not only by King Solomon but also by other ancient Hebrew thinkers. Scattered throughout the book are bits of wisdom that keep God's people on track. The opening chapter of Proverbs leads with an admonition to the reader about the fear of the Lord as the beginning of knowledge (1:7). The author then depicts wisdom in the form of a strong woman teaching the fear of the Lord to young men in the marketplace. The book of Proverbs concludes by proclaiming, "A woman who fears the LORD is to be praised" (31:30). Later, we'll look more closely at what is meant by "the fear of the Lord." Here, we simply note that both the opening and closing verses of Proverbs are about the same thing—living our lives wisely, not foolishly, in the light of God's purposes for us. In the first chapter of Proverbs we meet Lady Wisdom crying out in the streets of the city, calling young men to rethink their lives and their choices, and telling them to choose the fear of the Lord (1:29). Chapter 31 ends by putting Lady Wisdom in street clothes—a real woman, showing us what someone looks like who has wisely chosen to fear the Lord.

Surprise 4: Proverbs 31:10–31 is designed to be memorized.

The second poem in the chapter is unique in structure. It turns out that these last twenty-two verses form an acrostic: the Hebrew alphabet has twenty-two letters, and there are twenty-two verses in Proverbs 31:10–31. Verse 10 begins with the Hebrew letter for *a (aleph)*, verse 11 begins with the Hebrew form of *b (beth)*, then verse 12 begins with the next letter in the Hebrew alphabet (*gimel*), and so on through the rest of the verses matched to the letters of the Hebrew alphabet.

So what's the point of that?

In the ancient world, acrostics were used as memory devices. If you knew the letters of the alphabet, you could recall a series of ideas simply by recalling the next letter in the alphabet. We still use acrostics today in songs, poems, and books, but it was even more prevalent in the ancient world. Historians of Bible times tell us that virtually all early cultures (including that of the Hebrew people) were oral cultures. The collective wisdom of the people was passed down through the generations from mouth to ear. Most things weren't written down in books until many years later. People depended on memorizing what they needed for life. A poem in which each succeeding idea begins with the next letter of the alphabet was one way to help people remember the points being made.

Because most of us are literate and live in a world in which things are written down, we may think that in ancient times people in an oral culture would not be able to remember what they needed to know. On the contrary, scholars who study such things tell us that oral cultures actually promoted a high level of discussion, which aided retention. When we read something in a book, the sentence is there on the page, but we can't have a live conversation then and there with its author or with other readers. In contrast, in an oral culture, as ideas were discussed, they were vividly cemented into people's minds in ways we rarely experience today.

Proverbs 31:10–31 was written as an acrostic poem so that it could be memorized easily. It was designed to be learned by heart. In the process, it would be discussed again and again, and people would grasp its wisdom for living. That was true for God's people more than two thousand years ago, and it's true for us today. It's wisdom all of us need to help us live life wisely.

Surprise 5: We expect Proverbs 31:10–31 to be a reasoned argument, but it turns out to be a list.

We usually assume that the biblical text will build a unified argument as it moves through a group of Bible verses. We don't expect stand-alone ideas in a list. But a list can do us a favor in slowing us down, asking us to think more extensively about each idea separate from what precedes or follows it.

Lists have their value. I always have one in my pocket when I buy groceries. Otherwise, I'll return home wondering how I forgot to pick up milk or eggs. But other kinds of lists can be frustrating. More often than not, these are long lists of things I know I need to do. They can create guilt, especially when I've spent time working on a jigsaw puzzle rather than cleaning out an overloaded closet. Or such lists may reflect promises I've made or resolutions I know are important. I write those lists to keep myself from allowing the secondary to get in the way of things I know I need to consider primary.

Some lists can be handled quickly. That happens when I cruise the aisles of my local supermarket. If I check my grocery list before heading to the checkout stand, I probably have dealt with everything on that list. But other lists take days, sometimes even weeks or years, to work through. When it comes to the list that is Proverbs 31:10–31, I could choose to treat it as a quick list, one that simply takes a few moments to read. But when I get down to a serious consideration of these verses, it turns out that no single sermon can grasp and explore this list of verses in one shot.

The teacher of preachers was right. Preaching through a list is frustratingly difficult. And if that list is an acrostic poem meant to be memorized and discussed over a campfire in the woods or on stools in a local Starbucks, a sermon can make light of what is profound, or it can miss the point entirely. We don't want that to happen. That could lead women to set aside their gifts and settle for a lifetime of making daisy chains.

Don't get me wrong. Daisy chains have a legitimate place in our days. When a celebration calls for decorating our world, by all means, make daisy chains. But Proverbs 31 also calls us to make full use of all the gifts God has given us. When we choose to do that, we experience fulfillment, joy, satisfaction, and peace. Celebrate with verve. Then move on. Embrace God's gifts and calling. With Proverbs 31 as your guide, you can answer the call to live your best life. Join a host of others who want nothing less than a life guided by God's wisdom. That choice will lead to a strength and joy unrivaled by any lesser choices.

So let's dive into this treasure of Scripture. We may be in for a big surprise when we discover how practical and wonderfully encouraging the wisdom of God can be. On second thought, perhaps we should erect a BEWARE sign right here—to warn us that our study may change us and change much we thought we knew about what it means to be a woman of strength.

Lord, I am depending on your Holy Spirit to open my mind to the truth you want me to grasp. Help me to keep an open heart and an open mind as I seek to become a woman of strength. Amen.

For Reflection or Discussion

1. What difference, if any, does it make for you that Proverbs 31 was not addressed to a woman?

2. How have past teachings on the Proverbs 31 woman affected your opinion of her?

3. Why do you think a woman was chosen as the example of a wise life well lived in Proverbs 31?

4. In what ways is it important to you to be a woman of strength?

2

Becoming a Woman of Strength

Who can find a [*hayil woman*]?
She is more precious than rubies.

Proverbs 31:10 NLT

Years ago, while living and working in Paris, France, I attended a luncheon that was attended by both French women and women in the international community. The speaker at the luncheon was an American who addressed the group in English. In her talk, she mentioned some friends getting together for a chili supper. Now, all of us Americans knew immediately what was on the menu for that meal. Chili is part of American cuisine in a dozen forms—there's chili made with beef, chili made with chicken, chili made without meat, and on and on. But for the French woman translating the speaker that day, "chili" meant only one thing: something "chilly" or cold. So the French women in the audience heard that the Americans were having "a cold meal." This mistranslation didn't materially affect the women who heard it. Whether the meal was merely cold or had chili on the menu didn't change the larger point the speaker wanted to make. But sometimes we can miss what we need to hear when a mistranslated word *does* change the point, especially in the case of biblical texts that affect who we are or what we're called to do.

Bible Translation Boondoggles

Any time we move between two or more languages, we risk misunderstanding the meaning of words chosen by their authors. One reason for this is that words can change their meaning over time. For example, the translators of the 1611 King James Version of 1 Thessalonians 4:15 put it this way: "For this we say unto you by the word of the Lord, that we which are alive and remain shall not *prevent* them which are asleep" (emphasis added). "Prevent" the sleepers from doing what? That gives a completely wrong meaning to Paul's words. Modern-day translators know that the word *prevent* in the 1600s, when the King James Version was translated, actually means "precede" today. Verse 14 explains what is going on: "For if we believe that Jesus died and rose again, even so them also which sleep in Jesus will God bring with him" (1 Thessalonians 4:14 KJV). In other words, those who have already died will not be left behind. This simply illustrates the way in which the meanings of words can morph over time, even in a Bible translation.

Another issue for translators is that many words have multiple meanings. For example, if I look up the word *forge* in a dictionary, I discover that it can mean a fraudulent imitation (such as forging a signature). Or it can mean a metal shape for heating and hammering, or it can be a furnace for refining metal, or as a verb it can mean to take the lead in a race. If that's not already confusing, the word also can mean to forge ahead on a project. Which meaning fits what I'm reading? That depends on a number of things, including the grammatical structure of the sentence, the immediate context, and the overall intention of the writer. This is especially important to keep in mind with biblical texts. When I pull an analytical concordance off the shelf to look at a Hebrew word, I may discover that it has more than half a dozen different meanings, depending on its context. So words can change their meaning over time, and words can have different meanings, depending on their context.

To complicate things even more, one translator can assign meaning A to a word, whereas another translator may choose to assign meaning B to that same word. In that case, how do we know what a word really means? Often, it's the context that sorts that out for us. When a sportscaster uses the noun *play*, it refers to an action in a game, but *play* in a drama critic's review refers to a story acted out on a stage. And there may be other common uses of a word as it is paired with other words: come into play, play of colors, make a play, word play. The translator needs to interpret the context correctly in order to understand the meaning and select the best translation.

When we come to the Bible, we also face another confusing factor. Like other living languages, the Hebrew and Greek languages used by biblical writers more than two thousand years ago have morphed over time. So even today's meanings of a Hebrew or Greek word might mislead us about a word's definition when it was used by biblical writers long ago.

Meeting the Proverbs 31 Woman

We face the problem of changing meanings over time when we read, "A wife of noble character who can find? She is worth far more than rubies" (Proverbs 31:10). The Hebrew word describing that woman is *hayil*. It's a common word in the

Old Testament, so it doesn't surprise us when it turns up in verse 10. The problem is how translators have treated it. Back four centuries ago, when the translators of the King James Version of the Bible came to that Hebrew word, they decided that it meant "virtuous": "Who can find a *virtuous* woman? For her price is far above rubies." Here, we are face-to-face with a word whose meaning has changed over the centuries.

The word *virtuous* actually comes from the Latin word *vir*, meaning "man." While the translators did not ask, "Who can find a manly woman?" the sense of the word *virtuous* was completely different in the early seventeenth century: it referred to "a woman of manly excellence." What would have qualified a woman to be known as "a woman of manly excellence"? The seventeenth century produced numerous educated women who excelled in male venues. For example, Margaret Fell, the mother of Quakerism, was considered one of the "Valiant Sixty" early Quaker preachers and missionaries. Lady Margaret Cavendish, Duchess of Newcastle-on-Tyne, excelled as a philosopher, poet, scientist, and playwright. These and many others would have qualified as "manly women." But as the word *virtuous* was carried forward over the intervening centuries, it lost its original connection to the strength of a man, becoming instead a synonym for *chaste*. For several centuries thereafter, preachers have explored the text strictly in the light of that female virtue, chastity.

A hundred years ago, the King James Version of the Bible was the only translation most English-speaking Christians owned. But in the last fifty years, Bible scholars have produced at least a dozen new translations of the Bible in English. So how have they handled the Hebrew word *hayil* in newer versions of the Bible?

When translators of the New International Version (NIV) came to the Hebrew word *hayil*, they chose to translate the verse, "A wife of *noble character* who can find?" (Notice that while the King James translators spoke of a "woman," the NIV translators narrowed it to a "wife" because her husband is mentioned in the next verse.) The New Revised Standard Version asks, "A *capable* wife, who can find?" The Common English Bible asks, "A *competent wife,* who can find her?" The 1977 New American Standard Bible translators chose to ask, "An *excellent* wife who can find?" whereas the Contemporary English Version translates the verse, "A *truly good* wife is the most precious treasure a man can find!"

So what kind of woman is worth "far more than rubies"? Is it that she is virtuous? Or that she has a noble character? Or that she is capable? Or excellent? Or merely that she is truly good? As we think about this array of descriptions translating the Hebrew word *hayil,* we get some sense of how differently various translators understood this sentence. What is obvious is that the various translation choices do not necessarily carry the same meaning. Being "virtuous" is not the same as being "capable." Nor does it have the same sense as being "excellent." So what *does* the Hebrew word mean?

The 1917 Jewish translation of the Hebrew Bible into English came much closer to the sense of *hayil* when the translators chose the word "valor." Merriam-Webster defines valor as "strength of mind or spirit that enables a person to encounter danger with firmness; personal bravery." That definition has a very different sense from words such as *virtuous* or *chaste, capable, excellent,* or *truly good.*

But when we consult an analytical concordance, we find that the basic and most frequent meaning of *hayil* is strength, might, force, or power. In many cases, it refers to military prowess. In more than fifty instances in the Old Testament, the word described armies. A *hayil* soldier stands firm in battle, refusing to desert his post or to run away. One of the stellar examples of men who were *hayil* in the Old Testament is found in 2 Samuel 23:14–17. You may recall that though David had been anointed as the next king of Israel, the reigning king, Saul, would have none of it. With his army, he chased David and his band of men all over the desert wilderness southeast of Jerusalem. At one point, David was holed up in a cave with his followers who heard him lament, "If only I had a drink of water from the well in Bethlehem!"

That was all his finest fighters needed to hear. Risking their lives, they slipped through the enemy lines into Bethlehem and brought water back to their beloved leader. David was so overwhelmed by the willingness of these men to take their lives in their hands simply to bring him that longed-for drink that he poured out the water as a thanksgiving offering to God.

The three who carried out that daring quest are known as "David's *mighty* men," and the word describing them as "mighty" is *hayil*. Valor, strength, zeal, might—these are some primary ways in which *hayil* must be translated. The word tells us about the commitment of these "mighty men of valor." Throughout the Old Testament, the word is often translated "valiant." It describes a person who has an inner strength to carry through on responsibilities and to overcome obstacles. Proverbs 31:10 is about this kind of person.

Does Gender Change a Word's Meaning?

While the word *hayil* appears 246 times in the Old Testament, only 3 times did modern translators chose to render it as "virtuous" (or "capable," "excellent," "truly good"). In each case, they've made that change because the subject happens to be a woman. Is it that translators thought women couldn't be strong or valiant? Or that such terms simply did not fit their idea of womanhood? We have only to backtrack to verse 3 in Proverbs 31 to find the same word translated as "strength" when it refers to King Lemuel. There, the king's mother admonishes him: "Do not spend your strength [*hayil*] on women, your vigor on those who ruin kings." If the word can be translated as "strength" in verse 3, why must it be changed to "virtuous" (or any other word) in verse 10?

The three times that change is made are found in Ruth 3:11, Proverbs 12:4, and Proverbs 31:10. When we explore the Ruth text, we can see how unnecessary, even wrong, that change is. If you know the real-life story of Ruth, you know it's a strong argument for translating *hayil* as "strength," regardless of gender. Somehow, soft words such as "virtuous" or "noble" just aren't strong enough to characterize a woman such as Ruth. Think about the strength of character required to do what she did.

During a famine, a Hebrew family in Bethlehem had left home and had moved to the neighboring country of Moab in search of food. In time, they settled there and eventually the two sons married Moabite women (Orpah and Ruth). Then over time, the father and both sons died, leaving three widows. At that point, the widowed mother-in-law, Naomi, decided to return to her ancestral home of Bethlehem. So she counseled her two Moabite daughters-in-law to return to their fathers' houses where new marriages could be arranged for them. Orpah saw the wisdom in that advice and chose to stay in Moab, but Ruth refused to abandon her mother-in-law who now had no human resources to survive on her own.

Ruth's determination is clear in her declaration to Naomi, "Don't urge me to leave you or to turn back from you. Where you go, I will go and where you stay I will stay. Your people will be my people, and your God my God. Where you die I will die, and there I will be buried. May the LORD deal with me, be it ever so severely, if even death separates you and me" (Ruth 1:16–17). So Ruth returned to Bethlehem with Naomi, knowing that as a despised Moabite, an immigrant, she would be looked down upon. But she also knew that finding food to sustain the two of them would depend entirely on her.

Once the two women had moved back to Bethlehem, the text introduces us to a third person: "Now Naomi had a relative on her husband's side, a man of standing from the clan of Elimelek, whose name was Boaz" (2:1). The barley harvest had begun, and Ruth asked permission to glean on Boaz's farm. A gleaner's job was to crawl on hands and knees behind the reapers, picking up any bits of grain that had somehow been left behind. When Boaz visited his farm, he spotted Ruth on her hands and knees following the reapers. He was so impressed by this evidence of her commitment to her mother-in-law that he asked his overseers about her, and then determined to help her. When the day ended, he called to her and proceeded to load her down with grain.

We're not surprised by Ruth's response to Boaz's generosity: "At this she bowed down with her face to the ground. She asked him, 'Why have I found such favor in your eyes that you notice me—a foreigner?'" (2:10). But astute Boaz replied, "I've been told all about what you have done for your mother-in-law since the death of your husband—how you left your father and mother and your homeland and came to live with a people you did not know before. May the LORD repay you for what you have done" (2:11–12). That evening when Ruth was able to take a large quantity of grain back to Naomi, the mental wheels in her mother-in-law's head had begun to turn. Several months later, she arranged for Ruth to have a midnight conversation with her benefactor in which she would propose marriage to him.

What? Yes, with grit, faith, and determination, Naomi suggested a plan in which Ruth would ask Boaz to marry her. How "virtuous" does that sound?

Boaz responds to Ruth's marriage proposal in these words: "I will do for you all you ask. All the people of my town know that you are a [*hayil*] woman" (3:11). (If you don't know how this story ends, you can read Ruth chapter 4 for the conclusion.) Listen again to Boaz's words: "All the people of my town know that you are a [*hayil*] woman." So when translators of Proverbs 31:10 changed the meaning of the Hebrew word from "strong" or "valiant" to "noble character," we have to ask whether that's a legitimate translation made merely because the subject is a woman.

The first time we encounter a real Hebrew woman in the Bible who is described as *hayil*, it is here in Ruth 3:11. When we look at Ruth, we see a woman of strength, a woman of commitment, a woman of valor. The intrepid Ruth was more than merely "capable" or "virtuous." If Ruth's actions are in Scripture to tell us about the meaning of *hayil*, it's clear that the normal meaning of the word should apply to women as well as men. The shift from "strength" or "valor" to "virtuous" when the subject is a woman is hard to justify.

We might conclude that Ruth was unique among women, but even a moment of reflection reminds us of scores of other valiant women that we meet, not just on the pages of the Bible but also throughout history and in our world today. Consider, for example, a petite woman of "manly strength" named Mary Slessor. Her feats of daring and courage a century ago still astound any reader moving through the story of her life.

Another Amazing *Hayil* Woman

When I was a child, the stories I loved most were of indomitable women missionaries, women who at times went where men were unwilling to go, women who risked everything in order to bring the story of Jesus to people who had never heard of God's love for them. The nineteenth-century Scottish factory girl Mary Slessor was one of my missionary heroines. If any human being exemplified what it was to be a *hayil* person, it was Mary Slessor.

Growing up in the slums of Dundee in a large family with a perpetually drunk father and a physically fragile but spiritually godly mother, Mary at age eleven had to leave school and begin working twelve hours a day, six days a week, as a weaver in a factory. Rising at five each morning to help care for the younger children, then off to the factory for a twelve-hour stint, she spent evenings rounding up and teaching slum children both to read and to know God's love for each of them. When she heard about missionary work in Calabar (now southern Nigeria), she immediately volunteered to go there, to a land of pestilence and danger. Called "the white man's graveyard," few would volunteer for such a place, but for Mary it was precisely there that Jesus needed her. So in 1876 this *hayil* woman of strength sailed for West Africa.

What did she find when she debarked at Duke Town at the mouth of Calabar's Cross River among fetid swamps broiling under the hot rays of a brilliant sun? One of her early biographers, W. P. Livingstone, described the scene in these words:

> What a land was this she had chosen to make her dwelling-place—a land formless, mysterious, terrible, ruled by witchcraft and the terrorism of secret societies; where the skull was worshipped and blood-sacrifices were offered to jujus; where guilt was decided by ordeal of poison and boiling oil; where scores of people were murdered when a chief died, and his wives decked themselves in finery and were strangled to keep him company in the spirit-land; where men and women were bound and left to perish by the water-side to placate the god of shrimps; where the alligators were satiated with feeding on human flesh; where twins were done to death, and the

mother banished to the bush; . . . A land, also, of disease and fever and white graves.

There, too, lay her own future, as dark and unknown as the land, full of hard work, she knew, full it might be of danger and trial and sorrow.[1]

For her first eighteen years in Calabar, Mary worked side-by-side with the handful of missionaries in Duke Town, but her eye was always on the unexplored inland territory of Okoyong with its fierce warring tribes. At age forty, having often heard that no one could enter that territory and live, she wrote, "I am going to a new tribe up-country, a fierce, cruel people, and every one tells me that they will kill me. But I don't fear any hurt—only to combat their savage customs will require courage and firmness on my part."[2] This is a *hayil* woman in action.

The only modes of travel inland were by canoe through dangerous creeks and rivers, and then by foot through impenetrable jungles filled with wild animals, poisonous snakes, and death-dealing tribes constantly battling one another. Undaunted, Mary found her way to the town of Ifako where she charmed the chief by her fearlessness as she asked for a plot of land on which she would build a school. With much haggling, she was given that land, but meanwhile she would live in a one-room hut with a mud floor.

Almost immediately, she learned that when women in the tribe gave birth to twins, the infants were immediately crushed to death and the mother exiled to live (and die) in the jungle outside the community. Whenever Mary heard the sounds in the town that announced the birth of twins, she made every effort to save the babies and the mother, bringing them into her one-room mud hut to be protected from the community. In addition to the inconvenience of caring for mothers and infants in her tiny room, Mary also had to fend off the community leaders who were sure the presence of twins in town would bring evil down on all of them.

This small snippet of an extraordinary life lived for God under unthinkably difficult circumstances doesn't begin to carry any sense of the vision and hard work Mary undertook for the next thirty years as she continued to press inland, pacifying one tribe and then another, seeing churches and schools planted in town after town. Finding that shoes made trekking through jungles more difficult, she kicked them off and traveled jungle trails barefoot. She also tossed aside the confining dresses and petticoats worn by women at that time. Often ill with malaria or exhausted by the constant demands of missionary work, she pressed on into the Nigerian interior. Her integrity won the confidence of tribal chiefs to the point that she became the go-to person for negotiating disputes between tribes.

Livingstone gives us this snippet of her long and dangerous career:

> Mary could be as stern and strong as her native [Scottish] granite when combating evil. . . . An intoxicated man, carrying a loaded gun, once came to see her. She ordered him to put the gun in a corner of the verandah. He declined. She went up, wrested the gun from him, placed it in a corner, and defied him to touch it. He went away, and came back every day for a week before she gave it up. . . . She went and prevented two tribes from fighting; although her heart was beating wildly she stood between them and made each pile their guns on opposite sides of her, until the heaps were five feet high. On another occasion she stopped and impounded a canoe-load of machetes that were going up-river to be used in a war.[3]

This is Mary Slessor, truly a *hayil* woman. Like our Proverbs 31 woman, Mary had strength to carry through on her unbelievably difficult, self-imposed responsibilities. She overcame immense obstacles as the strong, valiant woman of God that she was. And like the Proverbs 31 woman of strength, Mary was "worth far more than rubies" (Proverbs 31:10). We may smile at the thought of this rough-and-tumble barefoot missionary being compared in value to precious stones. But that's a comparison worthy of any *hayil* woman.

A Woman Worth More Than Rubies

The Proverbs 31 woman of strength has what kind of value? The biblical poet tells us that such a woman is vastly more valuable than a handful of rubies.[4] Why rubies? Why not diamonds? In recent times, some large rubies have sold for upwards of $225,000 per carat. A comparably sized diamond sells for around $125,000 per carat. Why are rubies so valuable?

The Sanskrit word for ruby is *ratnaraj*, which means "king of precious stones." Others have called rubies the most precious of the twelve gems created by God. Apparently, ancient Hindus believed that if a person offered fine rubies to the god Krishna, it would guarantee rebirth as an emperor. Some ancient warriors believed that possessing a ruby would protect them in battle. We're told that many medieval Europeans wore rubies because they believed the stones would guarantee them health, wealth, wisdom, and even success in love! And what about Dorothy's ruby-red slippers in the legend of *The Wizard of Oz*? It was thought that they would protect her from evil. Perhaps these notions come from the belief that the deep red color of a ruby is like the deep red color of our blood, giving the stones a power over life.

Whatever the legends that have grown up around this precious stone, it is significant that this most precious of gems created by God was chosen by the Hebrew poet as being of lesser value than a woman of strength, a *hayil* woman. She is a person who is strong, even valiant. She has an inner strength to overcome obstacles.

As we walk through the remaining verses in this final chapter of the book of Proverbs, we observe a woman who has exceptional skill for living. We see what wisdom looks like in everyday life. As we examine the life of such a woman, we learn the qualities that summarize all the wisdom of the people of God. In the following chapters, we will dig into the specifics of what it is to be such a woman in daily life.

Lord, is it true that a Proverbs 31 woman of strength is worth far more than rubies? I'd like to be such a woman, but at what cost? I'm no Mary Slessor. I'm not always brave like David's mighty men. What must happen in my life to help me become the woman of strength you want me to be? Teach me your way, Lord. And help me to say yes to you as you lead me. I ask this for my sake, and for the sake of everyone around me who may need a woman of strength in their midst. Amen.

For Reflection or Discussion

1. Before you read this chapter, what were your impressions of a "Proverbs 31 woman"? How did you feel about those impressions?

2. What might be some of the downsides of being a woman of strength?

3. What might be some of the advantages of being a woman of strength?

4. Why do you think God's Spirit chose this subject as the conclusion of the book of Proverbs?

3

A Woman of Strength Is Trustworthy

Her husband has full confidence in her
and lacks nothing of value.
She brings him good, not harm,
all the days of her life.

Proverbs 31:11–12

Friendship is a wonderful gift. While most of us have many acquaintances, we most value the few really close friends to whom we can turn at any time for any need we have. When I look back over nearly nine decades of living, the faces I see in my happiest memories are of Monica, Aurelia, Dot, Betty, Grace, and a handful of other women. These are the faces of people I knew would never let me down. They would stand by me faithfully. Many of my acquaintances—both men and women—were equally trustworthy, but our life together did not move on the same deep levels. As I ponder this, I wonder what single gift my friends had given me that set them apart from many other good relationships. In the end, I concluded it was that they could always be trusted to do me no harm and to have my best interests at heart.

I remember the day in college when Dot challenged me about an unwise relationship I was pursuing, pointing me to the apostle Paul's command to "Avoid every kind of evil" (1 Thessalonians 5:22). Ouch! But she was right. I needed to hear those words. Years later, I thought of Dot when I read, "Wounds from a friend can be trusted" (Proverbs 27:6). She took the risk of challenging me because she had my best self in view. She could be trusted, even when it required taking a relational risk. When we turn to Proverbs 31:11–12, we discover that the first characteristic of a *hayil* person is that he or she is trustworthy.

A Trustworthy Person Is Consistent— Even in an Untrustworthy World

The immediate context for this trust in Proverbs 31:11–12 is the close relationship between a husband and wife: "Her husband has full confidence in her and lacks nothing of value. She brings him good, not harm, all the days of her life." Because she is trustworthy, what she does for her husband makes it possible for him to trust her without fear of being duped. She's on his team, not on his back. It's safe to trust her because he knows she won't pull the rug out from under him when he's not on his guard.

Transaction

Recall that King Lemuel has been warned about such women, the kind who "ruin kings" (31:3). The women the king (and others!) should avoid were those who would seduce him for what they could get from the relationship. Instead, he was encouraged to find a different kind of woman, one who

hayil - Hebrew - Woman of valor or Personification of wisdom -

would not take advantage of him, and who could be trusted to keep his best interests in view (31:10–31).

A man who marries a *hayil* woman knows that she is worthy of trust. He knows he can trust her to "to bring him good, not harm, all the days of her life." Note her consistency. It's not that she can be trusted merely on Tuesdays and Saturdays, but she is consistently trustworthy "all the days of her life."

The "proof" for the husband's trust resides in what she consistently does for him. At that point we might raise an eyebrow, asking whether her "trustworthiness" is based on being a doormat. But that is not a true understanding of "bringing good, not harm" on his behalf. Often, doing good can mean doing the most difficult thing. Just as my roommate Dot proved her trustworthiness by challenging my behavior, a wife can sometimes best serve her husband by challenging him when necessary. Giving in to his whims can be harmful. Trustworthiness in the form of bringing good doesn't mean always bowing to someone else's demands, nor does it mean never reasoning with or contradicting a person. Being trustworthy is a far cry from being a doormat. The Proverbs 31 woman's husband can trust her because he knows that she has his best interests at heart. Her trustworthiness is not an occasional gesture, but the constant pattern of her life and her relationship to him.

When a man and a woman make vows to one another in a marriage ceremony, they usually pledge themselves to stick together "until death do us part." That's a long time in most cases, and it calls for mutual concern for the welfare of one another. Marriages often end in divorce when one or both marriage partners act selfishly (often deceptively). But Proverbs 31:11–12 describes a different kind of marriage partner. This is about a *hayil* woman of strength. Such a woman knows that it is in her own best interests to act in ways worthy of her husband's trust. The Hebrew poet is talking about women, but it goes without saying that a husband also is called to be worthy of his wife's trust.

When we stop to think about it, it's clear that only a wise woman of strength could know what was called for in any situation. Is this or that situation calling for agreement or for a challenge? The Hebrew text begins by telling the reader that "her husband can trust her." At his very core he knows that at her very core she will do what is best for him. He has confidence that she will always do what is right. Their relationship can be a light in a dark world.

Living in an untrustworthy world, we may read Proverbs 31:11–12 and wonder if such trust is even possible (or desirable) in today's world. So much in the wider culture has worked against trust between husbands and wives. Comedians make jokes about the little and big deceptions spouses play on each other. "The battle of the sexes" has a long history in which suspicion of a person's marriage partner is played out sometimes hilariously, sometimes horrifically. In many cases, long-standing laws have created uneven relationships that ultimately have pushed people toward divorce. More alarming are recent statistics on violence between husbands and wives. In 2017 alone, for example, 1,527 women and 710 men in the United States were murdered by their intimate partners.[5] This level of violence has occurred even within Christian homes.

We would like to be able to trust not only those closest to us but also those we deal with in the wider society. But almost daily we see or hear news reports about innocent people trusting those who in the end prove untrustworthy. In 2012, the nation was shocked when sixty-four patients living in twenty different states all died in a nationwide fungal meningitis outbreak after receiving injections of a tainted drug. Researchers looking for any common denominators eventually found that all sixty-four people had been treated with a contaminated steroid made up at the New England Compounding Center (NECC) in Framingham, Massachusetts. According to FBI agent Harold H. Shaw, it turned out that the head pharmacist at that company had "failed miserably by cutting corners, ignoring warning signs, and harming hundreds of people with his reckless disregard for their safety. Dozens of unsuspecting patients died because of the tainted drugs that were distributed on his watch."[6]

While that pharmacist is now in prison, the reality is that we live in a litigious society because so many people are not trustworthy. So we hire lawyers and sign contracts and do all we can to shield ourselves from fraud of any kind. We assume in such a society that the persons we deal with will take advantage of us unless we are legally protected. In such a climate, when we read about the constancy of the woman in Proverbs 31:11–12, we may wonder whether complete trustworthiness is possible between us and anyone we have to deal with—in our families or in the wider culture.

What is it to be a trustworthy person in an untrustworthy world? Zooming in closer to home, what is it to be a trustworthy person in untrustworthy relationships? What kind of inner strength is required to maintain our trustworthiness when even those closest to us cannot truly be trusted? When the Proverbs 31 poet named trustworthiness as the first characteristic of a woman of strength, that tells us something of its scarcity in a broken world. It also reminds us that being trustworthy is the foundation of character on which any stable relationship must be built. And it takes strength to build and maintain it in the face of so much untrustworthiness around us.

We might be tempted to brush this aside because in our tit-for-tat world, we see few models of trustworthiness in anyone having to deal with an untrustworthy relationship. But in Genesis 38, we meet a trustworthy woman doing the right thing for a most untrustworthy man. Her name is Tamar.

Tamar, a Trustworthy Woman of Strength

Ruth, the *hayil* woman of strength who took great risks in moving from Moab to Bethlehem with her mother-in-law, in the end married one of the kindest and wealthiest men in the community. At the wedding ceremony recorded in Ruth 4:11–12, we read this blessing prayer for Boaz: "May you have standing in Ephrathah and be famous in Bethlehem. Through the offspring the LORD gives you by this young woman, may your family be like that of Perez, whom Tamar bore to Judah." Who was Perez? And who was Tamar? On that prayer hangs the story of a trustworthy woman doing what was right in her untrustworthy world. We find her story in Genesis 38.

The story begins with Judah, the fourth son of Jacob, choosing to move away from his Hebrew clan to the town of Adullam in Canaanite country. There—no surprise—he married a Canaanite woman with whom he then had three sons: Er, Onan, and Shelah. When Er reached a marriageable age, Judah secured a suitable Canaanite wife for him, a woman named Tamar. We don't know the details, but we do learn that in God's estimate, Er was an evil man (Genesis 38:7). He was so evil that God destroyed him.

Long before it became a part of Israel's law, "levirate" marriage was widely practiced in the surrounding cultures. That meant that if a man died without any heirs, his next-of-kin brother would be required to marry the widow and produce an heir in his deceased brother's name. (The practice received its name from the Latin word *levir*, meaning "husband's brother.") So when Er died, Judah ordered Onan to marry the widow Tamar. But each time Onan had sex with Tamar, he spilled his semen on the ground, refusing to impregnate her in his brother's name. Why would he do that? Onan, the second son, knew that if the first-born son had an heir, it would greatly decrease whatever he, as second son, could inherit.

By levirate law, Tamar was entitled to a son to carry on her dead husband's name. When God saw Onan's refusal to honor his brother and impregnate Tamar, he took Onan's life as well (Genesis 38:10). Fearing for the life of Shelah, his only remaining son, Judah sent Tamar back to her father's house with one excuse or another.

Years passed.

Then one day Tamar heard that her father-in-law would pass on a nearby road to check on the shearing of his sheep. She veiled and perfumed herself, then sat on the roadside in the guise of a prostitute. Sure enough, when Judah saw this veiled woman, he stopped to have sex with her, promising her a goat as payment. But before Tamar agreed to service him, she asked for a pledge of payment (to make sure that eventually she would get that promised goat). Eager for the sexual encounter, Judah handed over to her his walking stick along with his signet on the cord around his neck. After having sex with her, he went on his way, sending the promised goat and expecting the return of his signet and walking stick. But when no prostitute could be found, Judah wrote off the loss quietly to avoid local embarrassment.

Three months later, Judah heard that his widowed daughter-in-law was pregnant, a transgression punishable by being burned to death. But when he pronounced that sentence on her, she drew out the signet, the cord, and the walking stick, asking to whom these might belong. In that moment, all Judah could say was, "She is more righteous than I, since I wouldn't give her to my son Shelah" (38:26). She had a legal right to be the mother of Judah's grandchild.

As you read that story, you might wonder what could possibly have made her "righteous" and how that could translate into being "trustworthy." What she did hardly seems "righteous" at all! But we have to see her action in light of the levirate marriage law: Judah's treatment of her broke that law. When he sent her back to her father's house instead of giving her as wife to his third son, he denied her what the law of the land demanded: a husband and possibly a child by that son. In prostituting herself, she took the only option open to her in that culture. However, to get the larger picture of Tamar's action, we need to step back and put her in the context of God's specific expectations for the descendants of Abraham.

In Genesis 17:9–10, the reiteration of the covenant God had made with Abraham includes these words: "As for you, you must keep my covenant, you and your descendants after you for the generations to come. This is my covenant with you and your descendants after you, the covenant you are to keep." Judah was one of the descendants who bore that responsibility. The widow of Judah's firstborn son had an obligation to continue Judah's line. We do not know how much she (as a Canaanite) knew about that ancient Abrahamic covenant, but she, not Judah, took actions that supported it.

If we think about the character of Judah, we are reminded that he had grown up with a father known as "the deceiver," the one who had stolen his elder brother's birthright and blessing (Genesis 27). Judah himself was the son of a woman who had become Jacob's wife through deception. Again and again, Judah had seen self-serving dealings in the family before Jacob fled from Uncle Laban. Once out of the nest, Judah had moved away from the Abrahamic clan, had married a Canaanite woman, and had ignored the requirements (and thus the promises) of the covenant. Then in Tamar's case, this "son of the covenant" thought nothing of condemning his daughter-in-law to death and excusing his own behavior toward her. But in the end, he was caught in his own duplicity and forced to acknowledge that Tamar had done the righteous thing in continuing his line.

It's interesting to note that when Tamar's pregnancy was complete, she gave birth to twins, very much as Grandmother Rebekah had. And in later life, just as Jacob had supplanted his older brother, Esau, Tamar's second son, Perez, was the one who continued Judah's line. Remember the blessing prayed over Boaz? "Through the offspring the LORD gives you by this young woman, may your family be like that of Perez, whom Tamar bore to Judah." It's as if Tamar's twins replaced the two evil sons of Judah who were slain by God. Tamar's actions were righteous in that they enabled Judah's line to continue. (And what about Shelah, that third son of Judah? He drops from view as Judah's son Perez becomes the conveyor of the covenant.)

Being trustworthy can mean taking actions that are risky in the short term, but faithful to the long-term best interests of the other person. While Judah had withheld justice for Tamar and then later hypocritically denounced her action and called for her death, in the end he acknowledged that she had been the righteous one. She had done what was in his best interest as well as her own. The blessing prayed over Boaz several centuries later reminds the reader that Tamar brought Judah back into God's covenant with his great-grandfather Abraham. Tamar lived in an untrustworthy world, but her actions proved her to be the trustworthy one in this story.

Demonstrating Trustworthiness in All of Life

Recall that the word *hayil* is used most often to describe fighting men or armies. Tamar fought for what was right, taking an enormous personal risk (being burned to death). While the call to trustworthy action is often heard in the context of a marriage, it is a call that extends to the way we respond in all of our relationships. Would our next-door neighbor testify that we can be trusted? Would an employer see and value our trustworthiness in the workplace? What about our dealings with people with whom we vigorously disagree—perhaps about a candidate running for public office or a law about to be enacted? It turns out that being trustworthy isn't only about our behavior in a relationship like marriage. It touches every part of our daily world and often calls us to oppose what we know is ungodly in our culture. Like Tamar, at times we have to fight for what we know is right.

While Tamar's action succeeded, at times we may find ourselves fighting unsuccessfully for what is right. I have a dear friend whose husband has repeatedly walked away from the marriage vows he made to her many years ago. I've seen her pain. But year in and year out, I've also seen how she remained trustworthy in that relationship when most of her friends thought that she had no further obligation to him. It's not that she never challenged his infidelities. And it's not some sentimental case of "standing by her man." This was a conscious choice, made before God, that she would remain trustworthy to an untrustworthy man because she had promised that. Only a woman of strength could deliver that kind of resolve in the face of repeated unfaithfulness.

We would like to believe that ultimately trust would beget trust on the part of a marriage partner. In a broken world that doesn't always happen. The god of this world may have blinded the eyes of partners who take the good offered by a trustworthy mate without returning it in kind. In such cases, it is all the more important that a trustworthy person have the strength to do what is right in the face of deception, even evil.

Women caught in the web of deceitful relationships may have to fight for their own survival and mental health. Staying in such relationships in some cases may be the right thing to do, but not always. When her husband moved another woman into their home, expecting her to acquiesce to that triangle under their roof, my friend knew it was time (many would say *past* time) to end the marriage. She did so, and left her beautiful home with only a few treasured belongings in the trunk of her car. Our Proverbs 31:11–12 text is about a husband who sees and values the gift of his wife's efforts on his behalf. But in a broken world many women live with far less.

At the same time, if a trustworthy woman of strength finds herself facing enormous, ongoing personal grief from a deceptive relationship, that does not have to define her. Her shattered hopes may send her reeling for a time, but the strength to move on is possible. The crushing deception has come from one person, but most women have other relationships. It is there that other friendships—trustworthy friendships—show up and step in and help her rebuild her life. When my friend began a new life in a distant city, it was the friends she had made over the years who swooped in with love and concrete help that gave her the support she needed at that time. Never discount the value of a trustworthy friend, one who lets us know that we are not alone in our grief or despair.

It takes strength to be trustworthy. It begins when we see its surpassing value as we've experienced it in our time of need. It grows as we practice it. And it becomes full-blown trustworthiness when we're in relationships that demand it. Just as we build muscle strength by exercising that muscle, so we build the strength to be trustworthy by practicing it. Our woman of strength did just that: she made up her mind to bring her husband good, not harm, all the days of her life. As she did that, her trustworthy "muscle" grew strong as it became the habit of her life. It is the same for us. Practice makes perfect. We'll need that strength as we navigate an often-untrustworthy world.

><

Dear Lord, I'd like to be known as a trustworthy person, but when the people closest to me let me down, I just want to fight back. I want to kick them as hard as they've kicked me. The last thing I want to do is focus on their best interests. Please give me the wisdom I need to be a trustworthy person in my untrustworthy world. I know it's important, and it's what you want. But it's not easy and it's not always clear what that should look like. I need your help, Lord. Amen.

For Reflection or Discussion

1. What is your reaction to the idea that being trustworthy is a crucial ingredient in solid relationships?

2. As you think about the people closest to you, which ones can be trusted to keep your best interests at heart and which ones might not do so?

3. Which ones have good reasons to trust you as a trustworthy person? How have you shown that to them?

4. Why does being a trustworthy person take inner strength?

4

A Woman of Strength Is Diligent

She selects wool and flax
and works with eager hands.

Proverbs 31:13

Have you ever felt annoyed when someone sounded off with some high-sounding statement that was meant to impress you, but merely left you wondering what that was about? Sometimes it happens when a self-important guru on a talk show sounds off. Or when an aspiring politician wants to make an impression. Or it could even happen in church when a Bible teacher says something that sounds as if it might be important but leaves you wondering what on earth that was about.

When that happens, I usually have two questions on the tip of my tongue. First, I ask, "Is that true?" Whether I understand the statement or not, I want to know whether it's even worth thinking about. I'll think about a statement only if I'm convinced that it may be true. Second, I ask, "So what?" If this statement is true, what am I supposed to do about it?

As we've begun working our way through Proverbs 31:10–31, we've learned that the first characteristic of a woman of strength is that she is trustworthy. So we might nod and say, "Yeah, that really is important—to be trustworthy. But in real life, what does that look like?"

Fortunately, the writer doesn't leave us in the dark. The rest of the poem explores the multiple ways in which trustworthiness can be tested. Some of these ways are located in the home, in our family. Others are evident out in the wider world of our community and places of work. But all of them, in one way or another, let us test the practical benefits of trustworthiness.

Proverbs 31:13 gives us the first test of trustworthiness: Our *hayil* woman of strength "selects wool and flax and works with eager hands." What is that about? And how does it relate to being trustworthy?

The "wool and flax" bit tells us that this woman's work has something to do with the raw ingredients of wool or linen clothing. If she is to work those materials with eager hands, how does she acquire them? Does this mean that she goes from store to store, checking out what is available and at what price? Or that she has hunkered over her laptop checking out online resources for those raw materials? And if she does find what she wants online, how would she know that the wool or flax was of the best quality? Does she look for the brands with five stars? Today, we have resources for finding what we need that were obviously not available two thousand years ago. So we need to step back into the ancient world to understand how our woman of strength came by the raw materials she needed. Then we need to explore what she did with the wool and flax, working with her eager hands. Ultimately, it's all about clothing, as important to us today as it was when our woman of strength lived. But when it comes to the work of clothing ourselves, we have the advantage.

Hobbies versus Necessities

I'm not sure whether the craft of sewing or knitting were hobbies or necessities for me. Perhaps a bit of both, depending on the season of life in which I found myself. When I was in fifth grade, while the boys had shop classes, all of us girls were required to attend home economics classes for a year. In the fall semester we learned how to sew various kinds of seams using an old treadle sewing machine. Our goal that term was to make an apron that we would wear in the spring semester while we were learning how to cook. I'm not sure which I hated more—sewing or cooking. Then during the Second World War, we Girl Scouts were given balls of navy blue yarn and taught how to knit. One obligatory part of our work for the war effort was to knit twelve-inch squares that would be assembled into naval hospital afghans. Knit, purl, knit, purl—*oops!* Pull it apart and start over. I hated knitting as much as I hated sewing.

But years later, in the 1950s, when my husband was a seminary student, our income was next to nothing, and our baby had outgrown being carried around in blankets. She needed a coat, and suddenly those home economic lessons became important because we had no money to buy a ready-made coat for her. It was with a sense of triumph that I found a ten-cent coat pattern for an infant, a twenty-five-cent remnant of coating fabric, and some lining materials. Of course, I had to read the pattern instructions three times before cutting or stitching because I could not afford to mess up! But the satisfaction of making that little coat and bonnet for Susan actually turned me into an enthusiastic seamstress. My necessity birthed a hobby.

I especially loved finding the right pattern for a special dress. Then I would hunt for the fabric that would turn that pattern into something I would love to wear. Slowly, the dream would become a reality as I cut and pinned and stitched and pressed the seams that joined odd-shaped pieces of fabric into what I hoped would be a stunning garment. And if I didn't make too many small errors in the process, I might have had the nerve to enter that dress in its category at the state fair.

While I had a choice in whether or not to make my own clothes, for most women in other centuries or in other parts of the world, sewing was a necessity, not just a hobby. Think back, for example, to the pioneers who settled the American Eastern Seaboard in the seventeenth century. On the ship that had brought them to the New World there was most likely a spinning wheel and possibly a loom among the travelers' belongings. A wife didn't have the option I had of going to a mall, picking out a pattern and some fabric, and then turning that fabric into a coat or suit. The spinning wheel and the loom were essential for a family's survival in those early years. Furthermore, the whole process of preparing to make necessary clothing for the family started back even earlier—to the sheep or goats that had to be sheared of their wool. Or to the flaxseeds that had to be planted in rough fields with the hope of a good flax harvest.

Most of the early settlers started life in the New World by building one-room houses with a huge fireplace along one wall and enough room for a bed (shared by all), a table, and possibly benches for seating. But also in that house were the spinning wheel and the loom. During long winters, the whole family worked together cleaning and carding wool or flax, spinning the short fibers into thread, and then weaving that thread into wool or linen cloth for coats, leggings, dresses, blankets, or scarves. Typically, small children were set to work combing all the impurities out of the rough wool after it had been thoroughly washed. Sheaves of flax had to be soaked for several days to loosen the fibers. Then the sheaves were beaten until the fibers could be separated and combed—the work often assigned to older children.

Meanwhile, the mother worked at the spinning wheel, knowing just how to twist the spindle to turn short fibers into long strands, which the father then threaded onto his shuttle and slowly wove into usable fabric. All winter long the whole family worked together to turn dirty wads of wool or stiff sheaves of flax into fabric that would clothe the family. Whether we're talking about the Proverbs 31 woman finding the best wool and flax or the pioneer woman spinning short fibers into thread, little had changed for women over the intervening centuries. Turning raw materials into essential clothing for a family was not merely a hobby but was a vital necessity.

With that context in mind, let's follow our *hayil* woman of strength as she shops for the best wool and the best flax for her family's needs. Make your way with me into almost any town in Israel in Old Testament times. On entering through the gates built into the town wall, we might be surprised to see that the houses are packed tightly together. But then we notice that the houses on the west side of town are larger and not so densely packed. This was on purpose. The wealthier folks chose to live on the west side of the town to benefit from the west wind. It would cool their houses before moving east and picking up all the obnoxious smells of a community without modern-day plumbing. Exiting the town on its east side, the wind would carry off not just the stench of the town, but the added stench of the work done by men whose livelihood came from tanning animal hides or scrubbing, pounding, carding, and dyeing wool and flax. They worked in what was called a Fullers Field, usually some distance from town for a good reason. Not only did raw wool stink; it was usually full of grease and dirt. "Fullers" is one way to translate the Hebrew word that means "washing." And the task of washing all that grease and dirt out of raw wool required strong soap and patient effort. Few jobs available to men at that time created a more objectionable smell.

If our woman of strength was able to buy wool or flax from merchants in town, those materials had already gone through the long process to transform them from dirty, evil-smelling wads into clean-combed short fibers she could work with. What we do know from the text is that our *hayil* woman wanted the best materials, and she knew the value of what was available. When she had the right wool and flax, she then set to work with willing hands.

If we drop down to Proverbs 31:19, there we learn that this *hayil* woman "holds the distaff and grasps the spindle with her fingers." Exactly! The distaff (a long pole) holds the unspun wool and is often propped between the spinner's knees, freeing both hands to twist and spin the wool or flax. Spinning thread is a skill our Proverbs 31 woman had learned. Then in verses 21–22, we discover that she not only makes warm clothing for all in her household, but that she herself wears "fine linen and purple." So if we stop to think for a few minutes about the distance those results are from the raw wool and flax, we have some idea of the commitment she must have made to her family's welfare. Her options did not include a local mall with a dozen clothing stores seeking her business, or an evening spent on the internet checking out the endless number of clothing outlets vying for her cash and promising next-day delivery and free shipping. No, the clean wool or flax had to be spun into thread or yarn. Next, she or other family members would have to weave that thread or yarn into fabric that could then be turned into garments.

If we stop to think about this *hayil* woman's household, we know it included not just her husband and her children but also a number of servants and possibly other relatives. When the text tells us that *all* in her household are clothed, we begin to see the magnitude of her task. Consider all of the steps—from purchasing wool and flax to the spinning, then the weaving of cloth that could be sewn into a single, finished garment—and multiply that by all the people in her household who needed clothing. If we do the math, we begin to appreciate her dedication and the commitment she made to her family. No wonder her husband could trust her to do him good all the days of her life!

When I open the email chain on my laptop, I'm struck by the scores of sites making clothing available through the internet. Obviously, clothing is a big deal for a lot of folks today! We want to be "up to date" and we want more than one option in the closet for every purpose. Are we ever tempted to ask whether our obsession with clothes is somewhat misguided? At this point, we may benefit from asking about how God might view what we consider "essential" clothing. At the same time, we know that clothing does matter to God, and some of the Old Testament prophets used clothing as a metaphor for our relationship to or estrangement from God.

The Importance of Clothing to God

After Adam and Eve had eaten the forbidden fruit, Genesis 3:9–11 recounts this conversation: "The LORD God called to the man, 'Where are you?' He answered, 'I heard you in the garden, and I was afraid because I was naked; so I hid.' And he said, 'Who told you that you were naked?'" While Adam and Eve had sewn fig leaves together to cover themselves, we may be surprised by God's first action on behalf of the disobedient pair: "The LORD God made garments of skin for Adam and his wife and clothed them" (3:21). Nakedness has always called for clothing. God understands that and insists that God's people clothe those who are naked and in need. In God's kingdom, clothing matters.

In Deuteronomy 10:17–19, we read, "The LORD your God . . . defends the cause of the fatherless and the widow, and loves the foreigner residing among you, giving them food and clothing, and you are to love those who are foreigners, for you yourselves were foreigners in Egypt." Is it possible that the great God, mighty and awesome, actually and specifically cares about orphans and widows and immigrants in the land? How astonishing is that? God's people then were to "show love to foreigners"—including those who needed food and clothing.

Throughout the Old Testament, God took note of how people with wealth treated the poor. Speaking for the Lord, the prophet Ezekiel stated, "Suppose there is a righteous man who does what is just and right . . . He does not oppress anyone . . . but gives his food to the hungry and provides clothing for the naked" (Ezekiel 18:5, 7). In other words, caring for the material needs of those who are poor defines those the Lord considers righteous. In contrast, any mistreatment of the poor defines the unrighteous. Commenting on the actions of wicked people, Job observed, "The fatherless child is snatched from the breast; the infant of the poor is seized for a debt. Lacking clothes, they go about naked" (Job 24:9–10). Here, hunger and nakedness are markers of evil deeds.

When we turn to the New Testament, we're stunned to hear the basis on which Christ will separate the righteous from the unrighteous at the final judgment. To those who feel unworthy, He says, "Come, you who are blessed by my Father; take your inheritance, the kingdom prepared for you since the creation of the world. For I was hungry and you gave me something to eat, I was thirsty and you gave me something to drink . . . I needed clothes and you clothed me" (Matthew 25:34–36). When those who feel unworthy protest, essentially asking, "When did we do these things?" Jesus's reply is simple: "Truly I tell you, whatever you did for one of the least of these brothers and sisters of mine, you did for me" (Matthew 25:40). When, in Jesus's name, we offer clothing to someone in need, He sees this as a gift to himself, and He is pleased.

James, one of the half-brothers of Jesus, understood this: "What good is it, my brothers and sisters, if someone claims to have faith but has no deeds? Can such faith save them? Suppose a brother or a sister is without clothes and daily food. If one of you says to them, 'Go in peace; keep warm and well fed,' but does nothing about their physical needs, what good is it? In the same way, faith by itself, if it is not accompanied by action, is dead" (James 2:14–17).

When we take note that clothing those in need is indeed a big deal for God, it puts our *hayil* woman's work in a new perspective. Her work is physical, everyday work, to be sure. Each garment represents many hours of diligent effort—spinning, weaving, then stitching. But in God's eyes, every tunic or robe is much more. It honors each member of her household who receives a new garment. It honors her husband, who, with each gift of clothing to each person in the household, sees one more evidence of her diligence. Ultimately, she honors God as she cares for those for whom God also cares—and that motivates her to pick up that spindle with eager hands. Why? Because she knows that her diligence in everyday work matters to God.

A Nursery Rhyme Postscript

Many of us grew up on Mother Goose nursery rhymes, and while writing this chapter, I found myself occasionally humming this one.

> Baa, baa, black sheep—have you any wool?
> Yes, sir! Yes, sir! Three bags full!

One for my master, and one for my dame,
And one for the little boy who lives in the lane.

It was nice to think that even the sheep cared about a little boy living nearby. Then I found out that the original words had been changed. The earliest published record of this nursery rhyme from the mid-eighteenth century read this way:

Baa, baa, black sheep, have you any wool?
Yes, sir! Yes, sir! Three bags full.
Two for my master, and one for my dame,
And *none* for the little boy
Who cries in the lane.

Why give two bags to a master, one bag to his lady, and ignore the cry of the little boy? What is the purpose of a bag of wool? Once in a while, raw wool has been used to insulate an attic, and at times farmers may occasionally have used wool pellets as fertilizer, but in general, a bag of wool has one object—to be turned into warm clothing. That wool has no purpose if the bag is not opened and its contents turned into something useful. But the nursery rhyme's three bags of wool may also represent an addition to that master's wealth. In a world of contrasts between the rich and the poor, it's possible that the tearful little boy has a clothing need that will not be met. In that case, Jesus's parable makes clear how the master will be viewed at the end of time.

When our *hayil* woman took personal responsibility for assuring that everyone in her household had adequate clothing, she not only honored her husband; she also took seriously God's concern for the poor. She left no one in her care crying for lack of warm clothing. She proved that she could be trusted to purchase quality wool and flax, and then to turn those raw materials into garments for all who lived under her roof. She understood that "lazy hands make for poverty, but diligent hands bring wealth" (Proverbs 10:4).

It takes strength to be diligent. One way we can put legs under our trustworthiness is by our diligence to see that the "naked are clothed," not just in our families but also in our communities. It's easy to overlook the needs of folks we don't see every day, but God trusts us with the responsibility to provide for those who lack the basic necessities of life. Jesus reminds us, "Whatever you did for one of the least of these brothers and sisters of mine, you did for me" (Matthew 25:34–40).

Lord, it's so easy to get wrapped up in my own wants and forget the needs of others around me. I need this reminder that it's not all about me. My friends are pretty much like me—when we don't really look at folks different from us, we fail to see their needs. Open my eyes to ways I can be your hands in providing clothing for those who need that help. Amen.

For Reflection or Discussion

1. What does James mean when he writes that "faith by itself is not enough; unless it produces good deeds, it is dead and useless" (James 2:17 NLT)? Why should my faith "produce good deeds"?

2. How does "being God's hands" in clothing the naked honor God?

3. How do you think our *hayil* woman's work making clothes for her household proves that she was trustworthy?

4. What have been some of your biggest challenges in helping to meet others' needs?

5

A Woman of Strength Is Dependable

She is like the merchant ships,
bringing her food from afar.
She gets up while it is still night;
she provides food for her family
and portions for her female servants.

Proverbs 31:14–15

My thirty-something granddaughter-in-law Joy and her best friend, Leah, own and run a popular café in their town called Limestone Coffee & Tea. When I've sat in a corner of the shop with my latte and chicken salad wrap, watching customers coming in and out, I've thought, *Yes, Joy and Leah, you're giving me a twenty-first-century glimpse of the Proverbs 31 woman of strength at work.*

What does it take to operate a successful coffee shop? To begin with, either Joy or Leah must be at the shop no later than 6:30 every morning, seven days a week. By the time they arrive, their bakers have already been at work for hours creating muffins and scones and cookies (some gluten-free, some not), as well as four kinds of deep-dish quiches. But it is up to Leah to make sure that every ingredient for everything on the menu is available to the bakers and cooks every day. And either Joy or Leah must be on hand each morning to open up and get the coffee machines going for the first customers grabbing coffee or breakfast on their way to work.

Our Proverbs 31 text tells us that a woman of strength "is like the merchant ships, bringing her food from afar. She gets up while it is still night; she provides food for her family and portions for her female servants" (31:14–15). We might read that text and feel little to no connection between that woman's pre-dawn activities and our own lives today. The way many of us feed ourselves and our families in the midst of busy lives is probably a far cry from that of the Proverbs 31 woman. But if we think about it, the underlying principle is that a woman of strength is committed to the welfare of the people who depend on her. Everyone in her household needs food. And they need it every day. So our woman of strength must be dependable. It can't be that she's faithful one day and faithless the next. If either Joy or Leah could not be depended upon by the workers they've hired and the customers they serve, Limestone Coffee & Tea would soon go out of business.

Granted, most of us don't have an economic investment like a coffee shop that we must preserve by our dependability. But while we may not have put up the money to buy a business, most of us still do have obligations that call for dependability. If we are part of a family, we can't ignore the fact that someone has to prepare food, walk the dog, or deal with laundry. Someone must see that dishes are washed and floors are swept—or the place becomes a pigpen. That "someone" may not be you, but every person in a family has obligations in life for which he or she is called to be dependable. (Any mother who has had to pick up constantly after careless teens knows the price she must pay if she has undependable kids.)

Or perhaps we have a job for which we're paid a salary or a wage. If so, it almost goes without saying that our employer relies on us to be dependable. If we receive a paycheck, we are obligated to do the tasks for which we've been hired. And we're expected to do those tasks faithfully, daily or hourly—not just when we feel like it. A worker who comes to work only sporadically will soon be out of a job. An employee who spends work hours on personal business or is off regularly taking three hours for a leisurely lunch will end up with no paycheck. Like it or not, whatever our station in life, in one way or another we are expected to be dependable.

"The Greatest Ability Is Dependability"

When I was in college many years ago, one classroom had a banner strung across the wall above the blackboard. On it was written, "The greatest ability is dependability." At the time, I didn't really believe that, but when I later had a job and then a family, I got it. I came to see that our IQ or our gifts or our experience become irrelevant if we don't use them dependably. It doesn't matter how smart or how creative or how ingenious we are if we do not bring dependability to those gifts we've received from God.

Most of us may not have thought much about whether or not God really cares about something as mundane as our dependability. But even a quick glance at some of the wise sayings in the Old Testament demonstrates that God does care—and that it matters for us and for others around us. For example, for folks in workplace jobs, there's this warning: "As vinegar to the teeth and smoke to the eyes, so are sluggards to those who send them" (Proverbs 10:26). For anyone who makes a living off the land, the proverb gives us this word: "Sluggards do not plow in season; so at harvest time they look but find nothing" (20:4). If we miss the point of that proverb, perhaps this one makes it clearer: "Those who work their land will have abundant food, but those who chase fantasies will have their fill of poverty" (28:19).

It's simply the law of cause and effect: a good result is most likely to come from doing the right thing at the right time. Joy and Leah know that if they want Limestone Coffee & Tea to prosper, they must be dependable every day, not just on Tuesdays or Fridays. But you might be thinking, "Hold it, Alice! Even when I am totally dependable, things don't always turn out well. Those verses from the book of Proverbs may be true most of the time, but not all the time." And you're right.

Over several centuries, scribes collected the wise sayings of Solomon and others, later combining them into the book of Proverbs. We call these wise sayings "proverbs." A proverb is an observation about life in general; it is not a rule that applies in all situations. We may want to think that every proverb is a promise from God, but that misunderstands their purpose. They are *premises* about life, not *promises* from God. But when we stop to think about it, it's certainly not hard to see the wisdom in being dependable. Think of it this way—*un*dependability usually has a 100 percent chance of not working out. As Proverbs 20:4 notes, a person who fails to plow at the right time will have nothing to harvest. In other words, our greatest ability—one of the best traits we can develop and practice—is our dependability.

The Proverbs 31 Woman in the Kitchen?

In light of our text in Proverbs 31:14–15, what does food have to do with being a person of strength? These two verses tell us that a *hayil* woman does what is necessary in order to assure that all who are under her care will have food to eat daily. Once again, we remind ourselves that this woman doesn't have a fully stocked supermarket two blocks from her house. Instead, we learn, first, that she brings her food "from afar." What does that tell us? In order to keep food on the table for her household, this woman has to think ahead. She must evaluate what she will need well in advance and allow the necessary time it will take for those essential foods to become available.

Did you notice in Proverbs 31:14 that this *hayil* woman is compared to a merchant ship? Why that comparison? What do we know about merchant ships? While we might think of the Middle East as a desert, waterways included the Red Sea, the Mediterranean, and the Persian Gulf as well as rivers like the Nile or the Tigris and Euphrates. Merchants used these ships to transport all kinds of foods and goods around the region.

Wealthy ancient Egyptians ate well. Because the Nile River flooded once each year between June and September, its mud and silt made otherwise dry land so fertile that the Egyptian diet included onions, leeks, garlic, beans, lentils, radishes, cabbages, turnips, and lettuce. Melons, dates, figs, and plums often rounded out a meal. Folks living near the Tigris or Euphrates rivers in Mesopotamia also had a nice variety of fruits, vegetables, dairy, fish, and meats.

In contrast, while Israel had the Jordan River as the country's eastern border and the Mediterranean Sea on the other, its central highland spine was dry and could not provide such an array of foods. If our woman of strength wanted to vary her family's diet, she would have to rely on merchants whose ships brought such delicacies from other lands.

Some biblical scholars suggest that because the text specifies that she brings her food from afar, she actually traveled to buy delicacies from distant lands. Others think that she probably arranged for local delivery of foods she had previously ordered from other countries. Whatever the case, she did not have the ready access to foods from international locations that we routinely have in our supermarkets. We have the luxury of living in an "on demand" world when it comes to shopping for food. Most of us have financial resources that allow us to make instant decisions about what we might want to eat. We might microwave food from the freezer or opt for takeout from the restaurant of our choice. Or it's possible that we prefer to pop down to our favorite diner or pancake house. So it may be difficult for us to imagine what it must have been like to think weeks or months ahead and make arrangements to secure even the basic foods required to feed a family.

For our Proverbs 31 woman, even providing bread—the "staff of life"—for the family required thinking ahead. Barley or wheat had to be planted, harvested, threshed, and ground by hand on a stone mill. Then it had to be kneaded into dough (with perhaps honey or olive oil added). Only then could it be baked on coals in a clay-lined pit oven and become food on the table. We easily take bread for granted, and if we run out, most of us can make a quick trip to a nearby store for a loaf. But in ancient times, even with ingredients locally available, providing bread for a household required a dependable commitment to the time and work required for the process of grinding, kneading, and baking.

In verse 15, we learn that our Proverbs 31 woman gets up while it's still night, and we assume that she's getting an early start in preparing breakfast for the household. But in Hebrew the metaphor is actually almost ferocious: the text uses the image of a lioness who seeks "prey" at night. Scholar T. P. McCreesh explains this for us: "At the very least this word represents provisions acquired only after the exercise of great strength, prowess, and ingenuity and would seem to commend the extraordinary ability of the wife in providing for her household even against great odds."[7] That metaphor of a lioness removes all doubt that our woman of strength faced no real challenges in feeding her household.

We don't know much about a typical meal for an Israelite family living more than two thousand years ago. From biblical examples, we do know that more than three millennia ago, Jacob prepared a red lentil soup or stew for his father, and that most food references in the Old Testament are to bread, wine, and the occasional slaughter of a lamb that was roasted for special guests. We also know that when the Israelites escaped from Egypt and arrived at the southern border of the Promised Land, the people were promised that it was a land "flowing with milk and honey," and overflowed with grapes, figs, and pomegranates (Numbers 13:23–27). When Abigail defied her shortsighted husband by carrying huge quantities of food to David and his men, the load on several donkeys included two hundred loaves of bread, two skins of wine, five sheep ready dressed, five measures of parched grain, one hundred clusters of raisins, and two hundred cakes of figs (1 Samuel 25:18).

Think about that: bread, wine, sheep for roasting, grain for baking, raisins, and figs. A household out in the country might have a garden or some cattle, but the Proverbs 31 woman of strength actually lived in the city (Proverbs 31:23) where her husband was one of its leaders. She could probably buy the basics on market day in town, but some things would still have to be ordered ahead of time and from some distance.

So when the *hayil* woman of strength rose while it was still night in order to provide food for her household, was the menu typical of local produce, or did "bringing her food from afar" mean that she imported the kinds of food that would grace a king's table? We can only guess at what might appear at mealtime. What we do know is that her family did not go hungry! She could be depended on to provide for their basic food needs.

When Translators Differ

In the second chapter of this book we examined the problem translators run up against as they try to understand what early writers intended in their choice of Hebrew words. We meet one such translator challenge here in verse 15. The NIV tells us that our Proverbs 31 woman "provides food for her family and portions for her female servants." It sounds as if our woman of strength cooks breakfast not only for her family, but for her servant girls as well. But when we turn to the NRSV, we find a completely different understanding of the Hebrew sentence. There, our *hayil* woman is laying out "tasks for her servant girls." In any large household with the resources to hire servants, a responsibility of the owners is to instruct their servants in the specifics of each day's tasks. So it would make sense that our woman of strength would be assigning job tasks for the day to each of her female servants. However, when we turn to other translations, we find them pretty much evenly split in their understanding of the Hebrew in this verse. While the New Living Translation states that she plans "the day's work for her servant girls," a number of other translations follow the NIV. For example, the New American Standard Bible states that she "gives food to her household and portions to her maidens." What is going on here?

At issue is the meaning of the Hebrew word *choq*. When the fourth-century theologian Jerome translated this Hebrew word into Latin (in the Roman *Vulgate*), he or other translators gave it the sense of "meat" or "food." That would support the idea of preparing breakfast for servant girls. But several centuries earlier with the Septuagint translation of the Old Testament from Hebrew into Greek, scholars translated *choq* as "tasks, work assignments." Which translation is "right"? It turns out that most choose to write somewhat ambiguously "and portions for her women servants." Portions of what? Food or work assignments?

When we check the word *choq* as it appears in Exodus 5:14, we find that it refers to the slave labor of the Hebrews in Egypt. On the strength of that example in Exodus, I prefer the New Revised Standard Version here, where the *hayil* woman's task is to give out work assignments to the female servants. Whether our *hayil* woman was cooking breakfast for her servant girls or was giving them their work assignments, it's clear that she understood that food must be prepared daily for all who were in her care.

Jesus, Dinner Parties, and Food for Thought

As I've sipped my latte in Limestone Coffee & Tea, I've watched people meet for chats with friends. Parents with their children have stopped in for snacks and beverages after a school function. A handful of teens makes a noisy entrance, then gathers at a table for a gabfest. I recently learned that one of my grandsons and three of his buddies are up early each morning for their run along the river, but they then end up at Limestone for very good coffee before going to work. Limestone may sell food and beverages, but it also provides a gathering place for social connection.

In addition to nourishing our bodies, food can also speak a language of love and care. Whether we eat it while seated around an elegantly set table in a posh home or while sitting on floor mats in a Bedouin tent, food brings people together. And when we turn to the Gospels, we see how food provided an important point of contact for Jesus and His followers.

When His disciples asked Him to teach them how to pray, following the prayers for God's kingdom, the first earthly request Jesus names in the Lord's Prayer is about food: "Give us each day our daily bread" (Luke 11:3).[8] (Theologian and linguist Kenneth Bailey reminds us that in that prayer we ask for *bread*, not cake, and we ask it for *us*, not just for me.)

Food and drink crop up repeatedly throughout the four gospels. Start with Jesus's first miracle in John 2. The seven-day celebration of a wedding was clouded by a shortage of wine. Had the host's family failed to plan properly or were the guests guzzling too much wine too quickly? Whatever the cause, Mary saw the host's embarrassment and asked Jesus to do something about the problem.

I'm impressed by the way in which Jesus required faith from the servants as he responded to the request for more wine. "Nearby stood six stone water jars . . . each holding from twenty to thirty gallons. Jesus said to the servants, 'Fill the jars with water'" (John 2:6–7). Water! Servants would expect water to remain water. Then came the second command: "Now draw some out and take it to the master of the banquet" (2:8). Take water to the master? How insulting that would be! But Mary had told the servants to do whatever Jesus commanded, so they did as they were told. We know the master's response: "Everyone brings out the choice wine first and then the cheaper wine after the guests have had too much to drink; but you have saved the best till now" (2:10).

The apostle John, writing about this, noted that turning water into wine was the first time Jesus revealed His glory. But other times when we encounter Jesus at dinner parties or telling stories about banquets, no miracle is in view. Instead, Jesus's enemies often used such occasions to attack His work. For example, in Luke 15:1–2, the Pharisees and teachers of the law condemn Him for eating and drinking with contemptible tax collectors and sinners. Eating with someone in that culture was an endorsement of those at the table. Jesus ignores their scruples.

Remember Zacchaeus? He was not a good or honest man. Instead, he was one of the oppressors, a Jewish tax collector in Rome's employ, taxing Jews for his own purse as well as for the Roman government. It's no surprise that he was despised by the Jews. When Jesus arrived in Jericho, instead of just hanging out with the respectable people (as everyone expected), He called Zacchaeus out of the tree in which he was hiding. Would He then give that man a well-deserved tongue-lashing for his dishonest fleecing of fellow Jews? No! Instead of seeking the socially acceptable hospitality offered to Him by Jewish leaders, Jesus chose to stay with Zacchaeus as a dinner guest in his home (Luke 19). Kenneth Bailey reminds us that the tax collector's house was defiled by the owner's tax-collecting profession. If Jesus entered it, then ate at that table or slept in its guest bed, He would be defiled and in need of some kind of ceremonial cleansing. Zacchaeus knew that and recognized that Jesus had given him sacrificial love—love that cost Jesus acceptance by many of the Jews. Understanding that, Zacchaeus would never be the same again.

Whether it was picking grains of wheat or barley while walking through a field or telling stories about feasts, Jesus used food and meals as teaching moments. Luke has given us a number of these incidents. For example, he records that, "One Sabbath, when Jesus went to eat in the house of a prominent Pharisee, he was being carefully watched" (14:1). That dinner gave Jesus one opportunity after another to offend the religious sensibilities of his host. After ignoring the Pharisees' "law" by healing a sick man on that Sabbath, Jesus noticed that other guests were vying with one another for the best seats at the table, a practice our Lord challenged out loud. If that were not enough, He then turned to His host and addressed that issue directly. "When you give a luncheon or dinner, do not invite your friends, your brothers or sisters, your relatives, or your rich neighbors; if you do, they may invite you back and so you will be repaid. But when you give a banquet, invite the poor, the crippled, the lame, the blind, and you will be blessed. Although they cannot repay you, you will be repaid at the resurrection of the righteous" (14:12–14).

Jesus then told another of His wonderful stories about a man preparing a great feast to which he invited his own kind. But when one and then another gave the host an excuse to stay home, he angrily sent out his servants to invite "the poor, the crippled, the blind and the lame" (14:21). If you had been that leader of the Pharisees when Jesus was doing and saying these things at your table, what would you have concluded? For religious leaders, the conclusion was clear—this iconoclastic rabbi had to be silenced!

Food figured largely in Jesus's teachings, culminating in a final supper with His closest followers before His arrest and crucifixion. Luke tells the story this way:

> When the hour came, Jesus and his apostles reclined at the table. And he said to them, "I have eagerly desired to eat this Passover with you before I suffer. For I tell you, I will not eat it again until it finds fulfillment in the kingdom of God."
>
> After taking the cup, he gave thanks and said, "Take this and divide it among you. For I tell you I will not drink again from the fruit of the vine until the kingdom of God comes."
>
> And he took bread, gave thanks and broke it, and gave it to them, saying, "This is my body given for you; do this in remembrance of me."

> In the same way, after the supper he took the cup saying, "This cup is the new covenant in my blood, which is poured out for you." (22:14–20)

Did the disciples reclining around that table that night grasp what Jesus meant by those words? Or, for those of us who "take communion" from time to time while attending a church service: Do *we* grasp the significance of bread and wine as symbols of Jesus's broken body and shed blood on our behalf? Or is it just another wafer or tiny chunk of bread or another sip of ordinary wine? We might not understand the nuances of the "new covenant" between God and His people, but when Jesus holds up a piece of bread or a glass of wine as illustrations of that covenant, the most basic ingredients of everyday life help us connect to its life-changing reality.

Food: Jesus's Teaching Tool, Our Daily Necessity

God uses food to illustrate the extraordinary truth of divine love. For Jesus, food provided an everyday illustration of God's care for us, even as it challenges us to take seriously our responsibility to provide for the hungry. When we stand at the kitchen sink washing lettuce or beating eggs for an omelet, we are handling more than just food. We're handling God's gift to us, the life-giving sustenance not only for us but also for those around us. It is our daily necessity, one we are called to share freely with those in need.

Ultimately, it's easy to fall into the trap of thinking that it was merely our labor earning money that made purchasing food possible. We take the credit for putting food on our table. But we would starve without the labor of an army of unseen folks who provide our food. From those who plow the ground and plant the seeds to those who tend the fields, to harvesters, to wholesale grocers, to our local supermarket, we depend on other people for our daily bread.

Joy and Leah do depend on the workers they've hired. But behind the day-to-day operations of Limestone Coffee & Tea are also workers in faraway places tending coffee plants or drying tea leaves. If those workers are not dependable, the coffee plants will die. At every step required to put food on our table, workers have had to do their work dependably. In a word, we depend on their dependability. But in the end, we depend on God who makes the sun to shine and the rain to fall so that crops can grow and people can eat. Praise God from whom this blessing flows.

Lord, how often I sit down at the table and eat good food and never stop to think about all the hands that made that meal possible. But when I do stop to think about food, I'm struck by how often you used a meal to teach us about your provision for us. I want to be more thoughtful about this, but it's too easy to forget. Every time I eat a meal, help me to see my food as your gift of love day after day after day. Amen.

For Reflection or Discussion

1. What do you think are the benefits of being a dependable person?

2. What do you think are the downsides of being a dependable person?

3. How important do you think it is to be able to eat with someone else, rather than alone?

4. What do you think are the benefits of sharing food supplies with needy people?

6

A Woman of Strength
Takes Measured Risks

She considers a field and buys it;
out of her earnings she plants a vineyard.
She sets about her work vigorously;
her arms are strong for her tasks.
She sees that her trading is profitable,
and her lamp does not go out at night.

Proverbs 31:16–18

Up to this point, our Proverbs 31 woman has been largely in her home, caring for the needs of her household. We've watched her make sure everyone has clothing to wear and food to eat each day. For some folks, that is all she needs to do. Doesn't that sum up the kind of person the Proverbs 31 woman is? So we may imagine her in a rocking chair, tranquilly knitting scarves for the family or out in the kitchen cooking a meal for the entire household.

But in verse 16 we see her stepping away from her front door and choosing a different role, one that might surprise us. We learn that she's in the country, away from her house in town, considering the purchase of a field. Watch her as she goes back again and again, thinking about buying that field and turning it into a productive vineyard. Would this be a wise investment? See her walking the length and breadth of it, checking the nature of the soil, noting the field's dimensions, and observing its suitability for growing grapes. She needs to be sure that the slope of the land is optimal for a vineyard. Will every square foot of ground get adequate sunlight? Is the slight slant of the plot adequate for good drainage?

As we watch her deliberations, we might wonder where the cash will come from that will allow her to purchase that land. It's one thing to have a dream about a vineyard; it's something else to have the resources necessary to carry out the project. Our text tells us that "out of her earnings she plants a vineyard." What does that mean? Then we read that "she sees that her trading is profitable." Hmm, so this woman has some kind of profitable business that provides enough funds to turn her desire for a vineyard into a reality. It turns out that our *hayil* woman of strength is also a businesswoman. She has her own financial resources, and she is now using them to buy a field and turn it into a productive vineyard.

Measured Risk-Taking: Investing in a Potential Vineyard

Let's assume that our *hayil* woman has purchased the field that seems suitable for a vineyard: it slopes gently at the right angle for good drainage, and in the Middle East it should get maximum sun exposure. But as she stands there, she realizes all that must be done to turn this empty field into something productive. She will need to have a stone wall (topped with thorn bushes) built around the vineyard to keep out predators, both human and animal. Then she'll need workmen to build a watchtower. Why a watchtower? Typically, these were built in the middle of the vineyard so that a watchman could see animals or thieves entering any part of the field. To build such a tower, workmen would pile up rocks and stones without mortar and then build a small room, roofed over, on top. Watchmen could then climb the rough stairs to that room to assure that nothing would be allowed to harm or steal the growing grapes.

Think about our woman's actions to this point. First came finding a field and then making sure it would be suitable for a vineyard. Then there was the matter of a wall. The land of Israel had no shortage of rocks but building a wall would require thousands of them—and the muscle power necessary to assemble them into a wall. She would have to pay the labor costs for that essential construction project. And then she'd also need a watchtower. Once again, it would take a major amount of muscle power to gather hundreds of stones and rocks and build them into a tower in the middle of the vineyard. Another labor cost. Only then could she begin actually planting grapevines.

As we think about what it would take to turn a vacant field into a productive vineyard, and we do the math tallying this woman's expenses, we may wonder about the extent of the investment our woman of strength will need to risk in order to follow her dream. It turns out that creating a vineyard is an expensive undertaking. And because it takes three years for newly planted grapevines to mature and produce a usable crop of grapes, she won't begin to benefit from this investment right away.

From these facts we learn that our trustworthy *hayil* woman thinks not just in terms of tomorrow's needs, but of her family's long-term needs. Would that include a need for a family vineyard? She considers her risks in making this long-term investment. She knows that it will require significant reserves of cash to turn that empty plot of ground into a viable vineyard. It's a risk, yes, but she also knows that with careful attention to every detail of the complex task she has undertaken, she should be able to succeed.

Risk-taking is part of everyone's life. Our choices from childhood on include risks of some kind—what to study in school, how to assess our gifts and commitments in order to choose a good career path, even the risk involved in choosing the right life partner. Some folks are risk averse: they avoid any and all risks where possible. Some other folks are prone to take risks that have little hope of success. It takes measured thought and planning to take those good risks that have the potential to succeed.

Matching Her Risk to Her Abilities

Note that our woman of strength *considered* that field. She gave thought to such a project. She didn't rush into the idea of creating a vineyard. Was this the best investment of her resources? What would she have to consider in order to succeed in this undertaking? Even with hired workers constructing the wall and tower, and laborers planting the seedlings and erecting a trellis system to support the vines, she had much to consider and then to do. So we're not surprised when the poet tells us that "her arms are strong for her tasks" (Proverbs 31:17).

But we might be misled by that translation, thinking that she was naturally energetic and strong. A more precise translation of the Hebrew text gives us a different picture: "She *girds* herself with strength, and *makes* her arms strong" (NRSV, emphasis added). It's not that she came by her energy and strength naturally but that she knew what she would need in order to succeed, and she *made* herself strong for those tasks. This is a necessary part of appropriate risk-taking.

In what ways would our woman of strength need "strong arms"? First, she'd have to have a clear understanding of vineyards, and she may need to talk several times with successful vineyard owners in her area. Then she'd need to know about hiring day laborers for the physical tasks of building a wall and a tower. She'd also need to know about varieties of grapes and their relative costs and productivity. In short, she would have to make her arms strong in every area in which she lacked knowledge or experience about creating a successful vineyard. The risks were there. But she knew what she didn't know, and she was willing to take time to learn what would be necessary in creating a productive vineyard.

Success in this life is often linked to what some folks call "long-range strategic planning"—looking ahead. When we first see this woman of strength considering a field, we realize that her mind was on the future, even while assuring the immediate needs of her family for clothing and food. We can take a page from her book. We might want to ask ourselves, "If I could do or be anything in the world five years from now, what would I want that to be?" Most folks who have accomplished surprising feats were successful because they could envision a future that in some way had enlarged on their present situation. We hear about those who grew up with very little, but through determination to get an education or learn an important skill were able to achieve noteworthy results. In her effort to create a productive vineyard, our woman of strength shows what it takes to succeed in achieving a dream. That dream was not without risks of failure. But she "made her arms strong" for the task. That is, she acquired the knowledge and experience that would allow her to succeed. We too can make our arms strong so that our dream can become a reality.

Turning Grapes into Wine

Once the vineyard was producing grapes, it would need one more piece of equipment, a winepress. In the Middle East, wine was always made in the vineyard in which the grapes had grown. No one hauled grapes to some commercial establishment for pressing and later fermenting into wine. So our *hayil* woman also had to invest in the construction of a winepress. It wouldn't be needed until the third year when that first crop of grapes was ready for harvesting, but building a winepress was a major task.

Vintners today use various kinds of machinery as the grapes move from the vineyard through the entire process of winemaking. But two thousand years ago (and in some parts of our world today), crushing the juice from the grapes was a social activity as friends and family climbed into the upper vat of a winepress and used their feet to stamp on the fruit. Where possible, winepresses were carved out of solid rock built into the side of a hill. They consisted of two rock vats, one above the other, with a few small holes bored between them. As people trampled on the grapes in the upper vat, the released juice would run into the lower vat, where it was stored until needed.

Given how unfamiliar most of us are with the ancient practices of winemaking, it's easy to read these verses about buying a field and planting a vineyard without having any sense of the risk, the faith, the knowledge, and the endurance required to make sure such a venture would be profitable. But when we look at this woman's massive efforts over at least a three-year period of time, we begin to grasp why she is truly *hayil*, a woman of strength.

Recall that the Hebrew word *hayil* throughout the Old Testament primarily describes warriors, armies, and military prowess. Like David's mighty men, it carried the sense of strength, might, force, or power. To be *hayil* is to be valiant, to be strong, to show courage or determination. Some dictionaries define it as being brave or fearless. In light of that, we might be tempted to disregard this woman as an unrealistic ideal, a kind of superwoman, rather than a real- life woman to whom we can relate. But our *hayil* woman wasn't just "born that way." The text is clear: "She girds herself with strength, and makes her arms strong" (v. 17 NRSV). She took all necessary steps to gain strength and to learn what she needed to know to assure that her vineyard would be profitable.

Counting the Cost of a Dream

Do you have a dream or a calling that will require training? Or an interest that is so deep in your soul you know you will never feel whole until it is satisfied? When you see these things in yourself, what are your options? Have you ever asked yourself what it would take to see that dream become a reality? It might mean going back to school and taking special training of some sort. It could mean giving up something in the short term in order to give yourself to something bigger with a longer-term reward. It's possible that it could include moving to a different location. It could mean seeking out others with the same dream and collaborating with them. Whatever the dream, it often means asking, "What will it take to turn my dream into reality?"—then taking steps to gird yourself with strength for that new undertaking.

Some of us are risk averse. Our fears of the risks required to pursue a dream may tempt us to think that we're born either strong or weak, and there's nothing we can do about it.

Or we read that the woman of strength stays up late at night or gets up before dawn, and that's enough to convince us that the cost of our dream is too high. Does this woman work twenty hours out of every twenty-four?

Old Testament scholar Ryan O'Dowd reminds us that the text isn't about long days and little sleep. It's about choosing our tasks strategically so that we don't waste hours on unprofitable activities. The psalmist put it this way: "Teach us to number our days, that we may gain a heart of wisdom" (Psalm 90:12). Did you notice that because life is relatively short, we need wisdom in our use of time? We grow in wisdom as we acknowledge the shortness of this life and then, in that light, we choose to live it wisely. Our woman of strength could easily have said, "It would be nice to have a vineyard, but that just sounds risky. I'll pass on that notion." No, instead she determined to prepare for the risks by making her arms strong for the task.

It is the same for us. The big dreams—the best dreams—require committing ourselves to the long-term disciplines that can carry us to the finish line. But this does not mean pushing ourselves 24-7 to get there. Instead, it's about making wise decisions and not cluttering our days with irrelevant activities. That commitment is one crucial part in making ourselves strong enough to realize our dreams.

Up to this point, we've been talking about a vision we have and how we might achieve a cherished dream. We have a choice. But sometimes the choice is thrust upon us. It is then that circumstances beyond our control force us to make our arms strong. That was the case for another *hayil* woman of the Bible named Esther.

A Consort Fit for an Emperor

Our woman of strength made her arms strong for the risky task of turning an empty field into a productive vineyard. But many women, looking at her, shrink from such undertakings. They've been brought up to see themselves in a different light. The idea of stepping out to change their circumstances seems not merely impossible; it may even seem wrong. This was true for a young woman named Esther. But first the setting of her story.

In the late fifth century BC, Persia ruled most of the known world and the Emperor Xerxes ruled Persia. He was a capricious tyrant and his will was absolute. God's people had been defeated years earlier and then the best among them had been taken from their homeland to live out their lives as exiles in a foreign land. Among them was a Hebrew named Mordecai, who worked just outside the gate to Xerxes's palace (Esther 2:5–6).

Xerxes had a large harem, and the first woman in that harem was named as Xerxes's queen. Queens at that time had no power beyond the beauty for which they were praised. A week into an extended banquet given by Xerxes for his nobles and officials, the king demanded that his queen, Vashti, display her beauty to the drunken men carousing in the room. When she refused, Xerxes consulted one of his advisors, who noted that if other women learned of her disobedience, it would empower them to disobey their husbands as well. That could never be allowed! So Vashti was banned from the king's presence and the search began for a worthy successor (1:1–2:4). Mordecai's niece Esther was among the beauties scooped up and brought before the king for his inspection. In the end, Esther was chosen, and after twelve months of beauty treatments, she entered the king's presence as his queen (2:12–18).

Meanwhile, the advisor on whom Xerxes relied most was an evil man named Haman. Each time Haman entered or left the palace, that self-important man had to pass Mordecai at the gate. Scripture tells us that, "When Haman saw that Mordecai would not kneel down or pay him honor, he was enraged. Yet having learned who Mordecai's people were, he scorned the idea of killing only Mordecai. Instead Haman looked for a way to destroy all Mordecai's people, the Jews, throughout the whole kingdom of Xerxes" (3:5–6).

What Haman didn't know was that Mordecai had previously uncovered a plot to assassinate Xerxes and had passed that information to Esther, and through her to the king. Sometime later, we find the king musing about how to honor the man Mordecai who had saved his life. So we have Haman plotting to kill not only Mordecai, but all the Jews in Persia. We also have Xerxes considering ways to honor Mordecai. Meanwhile, Queen Esther is in the palace harem, never free to approach the king, only free to come at his bidding. Haman seemed to have the upper hand, and it was not difficult for him to persuade Xerxes that a date should be set for the extermination of all the Jews in the land.

When Mordecai learned that such a date had been set for his death and the death of all the Jews in the land, he asked Esther to intercede with the king. But she reminded him that she had no freedom to approach Xerxes: "All the king's officials and the people of the royal provinces know that for any man or woman who approaches the king in the inner court without being summoned the king has but one law: that they be put to death unless the king extends the gold scepter to them and spares their lives. But thirty days have passed since I was called to go to the king" (4:11).

Can you feel Esther's helplessness in that moment? She had no access to the king until he called for her. We can understand this fearful woman as she saw no solution to the Jews' dilemma. But Mordecai would not accept her explanation. He fired back, "Do not think that because you are in the king's house you alone of all the Jews will escape. For if you remain silent at this time, relief and deliverance for the Jews will arise from another place, but you and your father's family will perish. And who knows but that you have come to your royal position for such a time as this?" (4:13–14). Quiet Esther could not imagine that she could make a difference for her people. But Mordecai's challenge pushed her out of the safety and calm of the harem and into the middle of a palace intrigue. Her discomfort was palpable. But her position as the emperor's consort could not be denied. Esther understood the risks, but she also understood that she alone needed to take those risks. Ultimately, she replied to Mordecai, "I will go to the king, even though it is against the law. And if I perish, I perish" (4:16). But she also asked Mordecai to gather together all the Jews in the city for a three-day fast, after which she would risk her life to save her people.

The three-day fast has ended. It is now time for Esther to act. Watch her, dressed in her royal robes, leave the women's quarters and make her way through the massive colonnades to the throne room. I suspect her heart is pounding and her mouth is dry. Then, approaching the king's throne unbidden, she watches as he spots her, then slowly raises the golden scepter to her, sparing her life. *Whew!* Her task at that moment is merely to invite both Xerxes and Haman to a feast she is preparing for the two of them.

Later at the feast, when the two men have eaten and have had their fill of wine, she is able to reveal Haman's plot against her people to Xerxes. In the end, it is Haman, not Mordecai, who is put to death, and the Jews throughout Persia are spared. What is fascinating as we read Esther's story is that in risking her life, she becomes a different person. Throughout the rest of the book of Esther, we see a woman of strength emerge from a woman who had merely been a very pretty but timid harem girl. Esther was not naturally strong. But because of the threat to her people, she took steps to make herself strong in order to avert a catastrophe.

Measuring Risk as We Choose Our Future

Most of the big decisions we must make in life come with some risk. Once we step out of our usual comfort zone in order to tackle something new, we are in risk-country. But it is there that we discover how much more inner strength we actually have. Like the Little Engine that could, we find that we're capable of more than we had believed possible.

Such situations in life often require that we make our arms strong. Sometimes we have a dream for which we need strong arms. Other times, we may face a threat for which we also need to make our arms strong. Like Esther, we may face a devastating choice. It could be that someone we value has turned against us. Or that the roof over our head is being taken away. Or an accident has permanently disabled our best friend. Losses of one kind or another come to most of us at some time in our lives. What we bring to those losses depends on how we gird ourselves with strength, how we make our arms strong. Esther thought her people would be crushed by Haman's edict; instead, her cousin motivated her to turn an impending disaster into victory. We too can make ourselves strong as we face crushing circumstances; we too can find strength to rise above them.

Then at times we need to make our arms strong when God has given us a dream. This is often a goal requiring all the strength we can muster as we take steps, one at a time, to turn that dream into a reality. Take heart! Don't settle for "same old, same old." Grab hold of that dream and make your arms strong for it. Our history is filled with literally thousands of folks who have done just that. Their success in the past can assure you as you first envision and then achieve that dream. From the woman of strength, know that it's possible to gird yourself with strength.

Lord, I don't think I have "strong arms." But there are challenges for which I should prepare myself. Please help me make my arms strong. If Esther could do that, I can to do it too. But I need your help to know how to use my strength well. Sometimes I'm just scared to death about the challenges I face, but it helps to know that you will be with me as I tackle them. Thank you for the promise of your presence as I move forward. Amen.

For Reflection or Discussion

1. What are your thoughts about the three-year task the Proverbs 31 woman tackled?

2. How do you feel about taking risks? Under what circumstances would you do so?

3. How would you go about making your arms strong?

4. What advice would you give another woman who is facing a severe challenge?

7

A Woman of Strength Is Generous

In her hand she holds the distaff
and grasps the spindle with her fingers.
She opens her arms to the poor
and extends her hands to the needy.

Proverbs 31:19–20

Most of us live on a budget of some kind. For some folks, it really isn't a budget but more just an effort to keep up with the charges on a credit card. For others, however, it's a real budget in which income is apportioned ahead of time to cover regular expenses—a mortgage or rent, standard utilities, car maintenance, household costs such as groceries, internet, and so on. However we manage the income we receive, we make choices about how we spend it. We may have enough resources to be able to debate which is more important—buying a new washing machine or taking that trip to Hawaii. Or whether we should put a new roof on the house or upgrade our aging automobile. Of course, some of us don't have those options because it takes every cent of income to cover the basics. But others of us do have choices, and those choices tell us more than we might think about our values.

We've been looking at the Proverbs 31 woman of strength, this *hayil* woman who not only provides clothing and food for her family but also has a business that assures her of a profitable income. We may be surprised when we discover the choices she makes about how she uses her profits. What are the values that dictate her actions?

Making Connections between Values and Actions

If we read almost any English translation of Proverbs 31:19–20, it's easy to miss the connection between these two verses: "In her hand she holds the distaff and grasps the spindle with her fingers. She opens her arms to the poor and extends her hands to the needy."

It looks as if verse 19 is just about spinning thread, and verse 20 is only about helping the poor. But in the Hebrew text, her spinning and her spending are interlinked. What we find in the Hebrew text is what scholars call a "chiasm." It's a literary way of saying, "Pay attention! These things may look as if they don't go together, but they really are connected and can't be separated." In Proverbs 31, the poet uses chiasms more than once as a means of keeping seemingly unrelated ideas linked together. So let's take a closer look at how chiasms are structured and consider a couple examples from the Bible.

The word *chiasm* starts with the Greek letter *chi* which is written as "X," and in a sense, some chiasms look like a big X. Think about how you make an X: you probably make the first stroke on an angle from top-left to bottom-right, then the second stroke from top-right to bottom-left, crossing the first stroke. Let's label the first stroke as A and the second stroke as B:

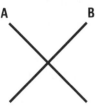

We can see that this X has four corners, one at each end of each stroke. Let's number those: we'll call the top left corner 1, the top right 2, the bottom left 3, and the bottom right 4.

Now let's consider a chiasm from one of Jesus's teachings: "But many who are first will be last, and many who are last will be first" (Matthew 19:30). If we plot this statement as the chiasm it is, it would look like this:

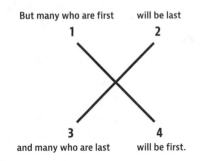

Corners 1 and 4 use some of the same words, and corners 2 and 3 use some of the same words. What we see in this verse is that the first and fourth lines are about "first" and the two middle lines are about "last."

With that in mind, let's look at Proverbs 31:19–20 with a literal translation from Hebrew that shows how this works:

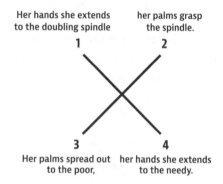

The diagram makes it easier to see that "her hands she extends" refers both to her spindle and to the needy. And that is what the poet wants us to see. The woman of strength works with the spindle not just to provide clothing for her household but also to have something to give to the needy. That's the point of this chiasm.

"So what?" you might ask. "Why does this matter?" It matters because whatever we do is usually motivated by something that matters to us. In other words, our actions spring from our values. This is true of big things as well as small things. Here's a very small example. I like our bedroom to be neat. So making the bed is one of the first things I do each morning after we've gotten up. Because neatness is a value for me, I take time each morning to make the bed. In the great scheme of things, does a made bed really matter? No, there are vastly more important things I make time for in my life each day. But what I value drives my actions—I make room in my schedule to make that bed early on.

Here's another very small example. My husband Randall and I value scheduling talking time with one another on a regular basis. So we have a coffee maker in our bedroom. Our workday starts only after we've chatted for half an hour over two cups of French-roast coffee. Isn't it a bit ridiculous to have a coffee maker in our bedroom? I'd probably have to admit that it is. But if I had to go to the kitchen to make our coffee, I'd likely be distracted by other things I need to do and our talking time would disappear. Being able to get out of bed, pull on a robe, then hit the button on the coffeemaker has a way of guaranteeing that we'll sit and talk a while. (It helps that we're both early risers.) We all make time for the things that matter to us.

Our Values Drive Our Actions

We also make time for our necessary tasks. And this brings us back to our *hayil* woman of strength. We already know that she acquires wool and flax so that her household can have necessary clothing. But the end product requires a time-consuming processing of the raw materials. Once they are clean and usable, the wool or flax must be spun into yarns before they can be woven into clothing. What we might not already know is that spinning was a time-consuming chore and more often than not, it was usually done by servants. Because this task was not respected, we're surprised when we discover that our woman of strength does it. And we might be even more surprised when we note *why* she does it—she spins so she can use her profits to help those who are needy. Scholar Mary Stewart Van Leeuwen puts it this way: "The hands that grasp [the spindle] to produce open wide to provide."[9]

As we think about this woman of strength and the connection between her work and her charitable giving, three things stand out. First, her giving isn't just a last-minute impulse because she happens to have some cash left over. Her desire to give is built into her work from the beginning. The chiasm linking her work and her concern for the poor makes that clear. It's as if the text includes a "so that" connector: she works so that she can give. We earlier learned that she works with wool and flax in order to provide clothing for her household. But now in verses 19–20, we discover that she also works so that she can provide for others in need. A woman of strength understands that she holds her wealth in trust from God. Proverbs 19:17 puts it this way: "Whoever is kind to the poor lends to the LORD, and he will reward them for what they have done." She sees her work in light of the larger scale of God's concern for the poor.

Second, what she does for the needy reveals her values. She values God's approval: "Whoever oppresses the poor shows contempt for their Maker, but whoever is kind to the needy honors God" (14:31). She values the promise of being refreshed by her giving: "A generous person will prosper; whoever refreshes others will be refreshed" (11:25). She understands that, short-term, she might not immediately benefit from her generosity, but long-term, it will matter: "Do not exploit the poor because they are poor and do not crush the needy in court, for the LORD will take up their case and will exact life for life" (22:22–23). God will ultimately judge her value system. Her attitude toward her wealth or toward the poor will receive God's scrutiny and judgment. She values her relationship to her Maker.

Third, the acrostic poem that ends the book of Proverbs summarizes all the wisdom of the people of God throughout the book. This woman's willingness to give to the poor echoes God's concerns not just in the book of Proverbs but throughout the Old Testament. She understands that "It is a sin to despise one's neighbor, but blessed is the one who is kind to the needy" (14:21). In this she stands in the long line of prophets among the people of God. What she does is driven by the whole of Scripture and thus demands our further consideration.

God's Concern for the Poor and Needy

Sometimes when Christians decide to read through the Bible from beginning to end, they move along well through Genesis and Exodus, but when they hit Leviticus or later Deuteronomy, the resolve to read through the Bible may crash and burn. It's all the minutiae about those laws regulating sacrifices, priests' clothing, and various kinds of offerings that bogs them down. And let's be honest, it's not hard to ask the so-what question at that point. Who cares what priests wore three thousand years ago in the Middle East? I get that. But if our Bible-reading resolve dissolves in the middle of Leviticus or Deuteronomy, we will miss some crucial texts that call us—in no uncertain terms—to be concerned for the widow, the orphan, and the stranger in the land.

God commanded His people to take two very specific actions concerning the poor and needy. For example, laws were put into place requiring farmers to leave the corners of their fields unharvested so that the poor could glean or gather the grain or vegetables there.

> When you are harvesting in your field and you overlook a sheaf, do not go back to get it. Leave it for the foreigner, the fatherless and the widow, so that the LORD your God may bless you in all the work of your hands. When you beat the olives from your trees, do not go over

the branches a second time. Leave what remains for the foreigner, the fatherless and the widow. When you harvest the grapes in your vineyard, do not go over the vines again. Leave what remains for the foreigner, the fatherless and the widow. (Deuteronomy 24:19–21)

Did you notice that three times God reminded His people to leave grain, olives, and grapes for "the foreigner, the fatherless and the widow"? In this way, God made provision for the immediate needs of widows, orphans, and immigrants.

In addition, each year God's people were to set apart one-tenth of their "grain, new wine and olive oil, and the firstborn of [their] herds and flocks" as an offering to God, eating it in the designated place of worship (14:23). At the same time, they were also told:

Be sure to set aside a tenth of all that your fields produce each year. . . . At the end of every three years, bring all the tithes of that year's produce and store it in your towns, so that the Levites (who have no allotment or inheritance of their own) and the foreigners, the fatherless and the widows who live in your towns may come and eat and be satisfied. (14:22, 28–29)

So every third year, one-tenth of all that had been produced in the fields, vineyards, orchards, and pastures was set aside to care for both the Levites and the poor and needy.

In addition, God also built a "sabbath year" into the calendar of His people: "For six years sow your fields, and for six years prune your vineyards and gather their crops. But in the seventh year the land is to have a year of sabbath rest, a sabbath to the LORD" (Leviticus 25:3–4). Farmers could reap what their fields produced for six years, but in the seventh year, fields should be left fallow. "Then the poor among your people may get food from it, and the wild animals may eat what is left. Do the same with your vineyard and your olive grove" (Exodus 23:11).

Perhaps even more surprising is this law concerning anyone who has fallen into poverty:

> If any of your fellow Israelites become poor and are unable to support themselves among you, help them as you would a foreigner and stranger, so they can continue to live among you. Do not take interest or any profit from them, but fear your God, so that they may continue to live among you. You must not lend them money at interest or sell them food at a profit. (Leviticus 25:35–37)

Furthermore, "At the end of every seven years you must cancel debts. . . . You may require payment from a foreigner, but you must cancel any debt your fellow Israelite owes you" (Deuteronomy 15:1, 3).

Finally, there's this command:

> If any of your people—Hebrew men or women—sell themselves to you and serve you six years, in the seventh year you must let them go free. And when you release them, do not send them away empty-handed. Supply them liberally from your flock, your threshing floor and your winepress. Give to them as the LORD your God has blessed you. (Deuteronomy 15:12–14)

Can we doubt that God was and is concerned for the poor and needy? These instructions go far beyond anything we might consider reasonable in our world today. And I suspect that they went far beyond what some Israelites considered reasonable in their day. So when we turn to the writings of some of Israel's prophets, we discover that a lot of God's people not only ignored God's rules for helping the poor or needy, but openly flouted them.

The prophet Amos wrote:

> This is what the LORD says. . . . "They sell the innocent
> for silver, and the needy for a pair of sandals. They tram-
> ple on the heads of the poor as on the dust of the ground
> and deny justice to the oppressed. . . ."
>
> Hear this, you who trample the needy and do away
> with the poor of the land, saying, "When will the New
> Moon be over that we may sell grain, and the Sabbath
> be ended that we may market wheat?"—skimping on the
> measure, boosting the price and cheating with dishon-
> est scales, buying the poor with silver and the needy for
> a pair of sandals, selling even the sweepings with the
> wheat. (Amos 2:6–7; 8:4–6)

Amos was clear: God would not tolerate that behavior for
long. A day of reckoning was coming. But meanwhile, the
prophet speaks for God, calling these callous oppressors to
"hate evil, love good; maintain justice in the courts," to "let
justice roll on like a river, righteousness like a never-failing
stream," and perhaps then the Lord God Almighty would
have mercy (5:15, 24).

At this point, we might shrug and say that good people—
God's people—would not do such things. God's condemna-
tion probably was directed only to the evil and godless folks.
But the prophet Isaiah challenges that thinking. Speaking of
religious people who meticulously follow the rules for fasting,
the Lord overturns their religious notions in these words:

> On the day of your fasting, you do as you please and
> exploit all your workers. . . . Is that what you call a fast,
> a day acceptable to the LORD? Is not this the kind of
> fasting I have chosen: to loose the chains of injustice and
> untie the cords of the yoke, to set the oppressed free and
> break every yoke? Is it not to share your food with the

hungry and to provide the poor wanderer with shelter—when you see the naked, to clothe them, and not to turn away from your own flesh and blood? Then your light will break forth like the dawn, and your healing will quickly appear . . . Then you will call and the LORD will answer. (Isaiah 58:3, 5–9)

Though many in Israel failed miserably in carrying out God's laws protecting the widow, the orphan, and the immigrant in the land, our woman of strength understood that "whoever oppresses the poor shows contempt for their Maker, but whoever is kind to the needy honors God" (Proverbs 14:31). She lived out her core beliefs, and in so doing, she honored God.

God's Goal for Us in a Broken World

So what do all of these ancient commands mean for us today? It would be easy to conclude that what was mandated for God's people living under the Old Testament law three thousand years ago does not apply to us. After all, we have New Testament teachings about grace, and doesn't grace trump the old laws? When the apostle Paul wrote a letter to the Christians in Galatia, he asked, "Did you receive the Spirit by the works of the law, or by believing what you heard? . . . Clearly no one who relies on the law is justified before God, because 'the righteous will live by faith.' The law is not based on faith" (Galatians 3:2, 11–12). Doesn't that relieve us of responsibility for things mandated for the Hebrew people more than three thousand years earlier?

Yes and no. In the first of his three letters, the apostle John remarked, "This is how we know we are in [God]: Whoever claims to live in him must live as Jesus did" (1 John 2:5–6). And how did Jesus live His life? After His baptism and the temptations by the devil, we first meet Him in Luke 4. Watch

Him as He stands up in Nazareth's synagogue, takes a scroll, and unrolls it to Isaiah 61, then begins to read out loud. When He finishes reading from that passage, He shocks His hearers by stating, "Today this scripture is fulfilled in your hearing" (Luke 4:21). And what has He just read from that scroll? Nothing less than these prophetic declarations:

> The Spirit of the Lord is on me,
>> because he has anointed me
>> to proclaim good news to the poor.
> He has sent me to proclaim freedom for the prisoners
>> and recovery of sight for the blind,
> to set the oppressed free,
>> to proclaim the year of the Lord's favor.
>
> (Luke 4:18–19, quoting Isaiah 61:1–2)

This sounds suspiciously familiar, and we can't duck Jesus's choice of texts to read.

Someone might decide that such a comment was a one-off, but when we follow Jesus around the Galilee and back and forth to Jerusalem for the feasts of God's people, we see Him acting in accordance with His calling. First, there are the miracles—the blind receive their sight, the lame are given strong legs on which to walk, the sick receive health, even occasionally a dead person is called back to life. But we also hear Him praising a poor widow for giving all she had even as He brings back to life the son of another destitute widow in need of her son's support. Then there's the matter of choosing to eat meals with despised tax collectors and notorious sinners (Luke 15:1). Some Pharisees might be heard muttering, "Huh! Hanging out with the wrong crowd, even with a rotter like Zacchaeus—that's hardly caring about 'the oppressed.' So much for what He says in a synagogue!"

But in addition to Jesus's actions, we hear the same themes

in some of the stories He tells—a story about a self-centered rich man ignoring a poor beggar at his gate and how the tables were turned when both men died. Or the story of a dinner party given by a wealthy man. When his equally wealthy guests failed to show up, he then commanded a servant to invite "the poor, the crippled, the blind and the lame" (Luke 14:21). Or that startling story about a king sorting out his countrymen, calling some "sheep" and the others "goats." We're shocked when that king praises the sheep and gets rid of the goats. On what basis does He make these surprising decisions? Then we hear Him state clearly what distinguishes the two: "I was hungry and you gave me something to eat, I was thirsty and you gave me something to drink, I was a stranger and you invited me in, I needed clothes and you clothed me, I was sick and you looked after me. I was in prison and you came to visit me" (Matthew 25:35–36). This sounds suspiciously like God's expectations for the Hebrew people a thousand years earlier.

Among the disciples who walked with Jesus during His earthly ministry, John "the beloved disciple" may have known the Savior most intimately. Reflecting on what he knew about Jesus, he later wrote:

> This is how we know what love is: Jesus Christ laid down his life for us. And we ought to lay down our lives for our brothers and sisters. If anyone has material possessions and sees a brother or sister in need but has no pity on them, how can the love of God be in that person? Dear children, let us not love with words or speech but with actions and in truth. (1 John 3:16–18)

Or hear these words from Jesus's brother, James:

> Suppose a brother or sister is without clothes and daily food. If one of you says to them, "Go in peace; keep warm and well fed," but does nothing about their physical needs,

what good is it? In the same way, faith by itself, if it is not accompanied by action, is dead. (James 2:15–17)

Earlier, James had taken to task Christians who favored the wealthy and looked down on the poor. He concluded that for followers of Jesus, "Judgment without mercy will be shown to anyone who has not been merciful. Mercy triumphs over judgment" (2:13). If we fail to be merciful, we have "dead faith." Even more, if we fail to show mercy, we should anticipate that we will be judged. That isn't a word we want to hear but hearing it may remind us that Jesus calls us to a concern for all those whose needs we see, whose needs we may be in a position to meet.

Acting on Our Values

It was the period of Lent, the forty days before Holy Week when Christians around the world remember the grim details leading up to the trial and death of Jesus. Lent in that church wasn't really about giving up chocolate or something else as a sign of self-denial. But the biblical text that Sunday had focused on God's call to mourn the state of the world, to pray for a broken world. The pastor quietly prayed. Others joined in—a businessman from India, a woman who was a seminary professor, a couple running a tree surgery company, a young Korean who played in the worship band some Sundays. I sat quietly, asking God to show me what part of this broken world should I mourn. Then I remembered a ministry a dear friend had begun—a halfway house for women being released from prison. Some moved into the house still dealing with addictions. Others had been in and out of prison many times and needed their time in the halfway house to be a turning point in their lives, a time to put the past behind them and trust God to give them strength and the will to live into a new day.

Driving home from church that Sunday, I realized two things: first, "mourning" something also means taking action to right a wrong, to address what we mourn. Second, God was asking me to mourn with my friend and her colleagues who run that halfway house. They were giving their lives to come alongside women the world had dismissed as unworthy. They mourned for these women and I needed to mourn with them. I could not close my eyes and my heart to women whose earlier poor decisions had landed them in prison. Jesus cared about them (Matthew 25:35). If I believed that, it called me to mourn the world that had turned these women into criminals and to mourn for each of them as they began the long difficult road to sobriety, to health, and most of all, to a new life in Jesus Christ. There was much to mourn.

But my friend also had recently run out of money to fund counseling and training programs for the broken women now living there. I needed to do more than mourn. I had promised I'd send a check I had recently received from a publisher, royalties from books I had written. But for one reason or another, I just hadn't gotten around to following through on that promise. My mourning needed to result in action. That check needed to go into the mail *now*, not next week.

We mourn the consequences so many people suffer in a broken world. Then we follow the example of our woman of strength who turned her work into a means of giving tangible help to those in need. She understood that God's gifts in our hands are to be shared with those whose hands are empty. She used her spindle and her loom to create wealth, and then she used that wealth on behalf of those needing food, clothing, or shelter. We know her values by her actions. Our woman of strength leads us to be generous with whatever we have in our hand.

Lord, I'm not rich, but I have enough food to eat and clothes to wear and money to cover my other essentials. It's too easy, Lord, to forget that there are those who lack the basics that I take for granted. Help me to order my priorities in such a way that I am intentional about sharing what I have with others in need. I know this is what I'm called to do with the resources that come from your hand, and I want to honor you by helping others in need. Amen.

For Reflection or Discussion

1. How do you feel about this woman's commitment to earn money so that she can help others in need?

2. How do you feel about the resources you have in light of this woman's example?

3. What are some ways you think it might be possible to help needy folks in your community?

4. How do Jesus's teachings and example help you think about needy folks?

8

A Woman of Strength
Addresses Future Needs

When it snows, she has no fear for her household;
  for all of them are clothed in scarlet.
She makes coverings for her bed;
  she is clothed in fine linen and purple.
Her husband is respected at the city gate,
  where he takes his seat among the elders of the land.
She makes linen garments and sells them,
  and supplies the merchants with sashes.
She is clothed with strength and dignity;
  she can laugh at the days to come.

Proverbs 31:21–25

From time to time when I'm reading, I come across a paragraph or two that I have to go back to and reread multiple times. Usually that happens because it seems that the writer has jumbled together several different ideas without any clear sequence of thought. If I'm honest, I have to admit that I've had that experience when reading Proverbs 31:21–25. Up front, I want you to know that without the aid of several Old Testament scholars, I'd still be in the dark about the seemingly unrelated ideas in this sequence of verses. How do winter clothes, bedspreads, purple gowns, civic leaders, stuff for merchants, and laughing about the future all in one paragraph make sense? From the scholars I've learned that together these statements *do* make sense. So let's dig in and discover what these verses are really about.

Poetry Then and Now

How do you know whether or not something you're reading is a poem? Nowadays, if I see words on a page in a fairly narrow column with just four or five words to a line, I can assume that I'm reading a poem. Teachers called that "free verse." Back when I was in school, we had a lot of rules about what made a poem "poetry." One rule had to do with meter—the repeated rhythm in a line. For example, when the early nineteenth-century English poet Lord Byron wrote about God's miraculous destruction of the Assyrian general Sennacherib, these were his first two lines:

> The Assyrian came down like the wolf on the fold.
> And his cohorts were gleaming in purple and gold.

Read those two lines out loud. Can you feel the rhythm Byron created using two short (unstressed) syllables followed by one long (stressed) syllable four times in each line? Those three-syllable units are called "anapests." If you were to read the whole poem out loud, you'd actually feel that anapestic rhythm resembling someone riding a horse into battle.

Or read out loud the opening lines of Whittier's poem "Snowbound":

The sun that brief December day
rose cheerless over hills of gray.

As you hear those lines, can you feel the rhythm of a short beat, a long beat, a short beat, a long beat? By the old rules of poetry, each line should have some kind of discernable rhythm or meter.

We're more likely to know that a poem is a poem if the lines rhyme. In Whittier's poem it's easy to see that *day* rhymes with *gray*. And Byron ended the first two lines with rhyming words, *fold* and *gold*. Even apart from the actual words, the way words are chosen to go together can create a mood in the reader. Poets could use both meter and rhyme to build a mood even as they chose words to express it. But the rules for poetry have changed over the last hundred years and much contemporary poetry does not rely on meter or rhyme.

Even more different from our ideas about poetry were the rules for poetry in other times and other cultures. So when we come to ancient Hebrew poetry, and in particular to Proverbs 31:21–25, we might think that the writer simply had a bad night, skipping from one idea or fact to another haphazardly. But Old Testament scholars put us straight because they can see that these five verses make up a brilliant chiasm. (Yes, another chiasm!) However, this time, instead of plotting the phrases on the corners of an X, we can understand them best when they are laid out like this:

A She has no fear when it snows
  B Her household has warm clothes
    C She makes bedspreads and clothing for herself
      X Her husband is respected at the city gate
    C´ She makes garments and sashes for merchants
  B´ She is clothed in strength and dignity
A´ She can laugh at the future

When we see a chiasm with an uneven number of lines and we lay it out on the page like this, it turns out that the middle line (in this case, X, "her husband is respected at the city gate") is the center point of the chiasm. There are other chiasms like this in the book of Proverbs. Three thousand years ago, such a structure was a distinguishing mark of good Hebrew poetry.

So as we look at this chiasm, what are we supposed to see? Well, we look at similarities between A and A´, then between B and B´, and then between C and C´:

- Having clothed her household well, she doesn't fear cold weather (A), which means she can laugh at the future (A´).
- She herself is clothed in fine linen and purple (B), which means she is also clothed in strength and dignity (B´).
- She makes coverings for her bed and clothing for herself (C), and she also makes garments and sashes to sell to the merchants (C´).

You can see the way the poet constructed the chiasm using the same words to express parallel ideas: she is clothed . . . she is clothed; she makes . . . she makes.

When you see the chiasm laid out this way on the page, it seems to resemble an arrow with the X-factor at the point of it. And that is precisely what the poet wants you to see—that the woman's husband is respected as one of the leaders of the community. All the things that occupy the work life of our *hayil* woman enhance her husband in his role as a civic elder. In fact, her work actually empowers him in his own work for the city.

If we think about it, how we choose to live our lives impacts everyone else under our roof. Our degree of diligence or lack of it is reflected in how others in our close circle may be viewed and treated. And any negligence on our part is also reflected in what others must do to compensate for our failures. So in this chiasm the poet is telling us that a *hayil* person's work has the possibility of empowering everyone around her. What we learn from this woman's activities can give us a sense of the range of ways our choices may impact our family, our coworkers, or even some neighbors down the street.

Six Pictures

When you were young, what kinds of things did you find easy to remember, and what was easy to forget? For me, stories usually stuck in my mind while rules or orders generally slipped out quickly. That certainly was true during my years in elementary school. It's also possible that we've had that experience when we read the Bible. So does it surprise us that, by far, the Bible teaches through stories and pictures? I always heard about the "teachings" of the Bible as abstract rules for living. Instead, I've come to see that the stories of people's lives instruct us sometimes more powerfully. In short, the biblical writers teach by describing things we can grasp with our imaginations as well as with our minds. We might think that the book of Proverbs just gives us "rules for living," but most of the proverbs are themselves pictures. Our chiasm makes its point in a series of pictures—of winter weather, warm clothes, elegant dresses, fancy bedspreads, high-end merchandise, a laughing lady, and a community leader at work. Let's look at our chiasm through the following six pictures.

Picture 1: A Family Kept Warm in Winter

"When it snows, she has no fear for her household; for all of them are clothed in scarlet" (Proverbs 31:21). The first time I read that line, I giggled. How often does it snow in the Middle East? I've since discovered that during the wintery season between November and February, it occasionally does snow in and around Jerusalem. Of course, the threat of snow there is nothing compared to the amount of snow we deal with each winter here in northern Illinois where I now live. But this woman knew that her household needed warm clothing in the winter months. When we're cold, it's hard to focus on what we need to do because we are distracted by our discomfort and we're constantly looking for a heat source to warm us. A *hayil* person understands that providing warm clothing in winter is vital for the health and productivity of those in her household.

I also giggled when I first read that the clothing kept them warm because it was red ("scarlet"). Then I learned that scarlet dye was expensive because it was made from a seashell found off the coast of Phoenicia, which meant that only the wealthy could afford red clothing. But I still didn't get how red clothes would keep a person warm in winter. Then I read that "scarlet" sometimes referred to a heavier fabric, perhaps made of wool, that would provide warmth in cold weather. So scarlet clothing was certainly expensive and was possibly made of a warmer cloth.

Perhaps these explanations are valid. But for a different understanding of what made this clothing warm in winter, other scholars point us to the Septuagint and the Latin *Vulgate* translations of Proverbs 31:21, in which the Hebrew word for scarlet was interpreted to mean "two-ply," that is, lined garments. Whether the woman of strength furnished her household with lined garments or those made of a thicker fabric dyed red, for us the bottom line is that she was concerned that all in her household be warm in winter. The clothing she made was warm enough to protect against the cold.

Picture 2: A Well-Dressed Aristocratic Woman

In verse 22, we read, "She makes coverings for her bed; she is clothed in fine linen and purple." If we think about this woman's output in fabrics, it's clear that she was adept in choosing her wool and flax carefully (31:13), spinning the raw materials into thread (31:19) from which she could weave fabrics, and then using the fabrics to create a variety of clothing items. We already know she had a profitable business (31:18), and from later verses we will learn that at least a part of her income came from the creation of garments and sashes she sold to merchants (31:24). It now becomes clear that the servant girls we met back in verse 15 may have worked in this home-based fabric-creation business. It's hard to imagine that even our woman of strength could have single-handedly spun, woven, and sewn all of the garments for her household, for herself, and for sale to the merchants.

More to the point, the clothing worn by this woman of strength marks her as an aristocrat in her community. She is a woman of substance and she dresses accordingly. "Fine linen" was usually imported from Egypt. The flax growing along the Nile River produced a fabric almost silky to the touch and whiter than linens created from flax plants grown elsewhere. To wear garments made from such fine linen befitted a woman in her position.

This brings up a point worth noting: it is only here in the entire poem that we find any reference to this woman's care for herself. Because we've seen her devoting her energies to her household and to those in need, we might assume that self-denial or self-disregard is a desirable virtue. It could appear that ignoring one's appearance is "spiritual." Not so. As the wife of one of the leaders of the city, how she dressed mattered. Caring for her personal appearance was as important to her husband's honor as assuring that her household was warmly dressed in winter.

Picture 3: A Community Leader Freed to Lead

That brings us to the central point of this chiasm: "Her husband is respected at the city gate." Most of us are familiar with gates. We use gates to keep out unwanted traffic. A gate keeps a pet inside a yard or keeps people in line at a stadium. In Old Testament times, a city gate was the one opening in the high wall built around a town for protection from enemies. It was often open during daylight hours, but closed tightly at dusk. And when enemies wanted entrance to the town or city, the gate was strong enough to keep them out. So the first function of the city gate was to control who could enter the community.

The city gate also had other important functions. In peacetime, merchants often set up their stalls at the gate. Farmers brought in produce to sell at the gate. It was a noisy place with all the bartering required to purchase food, leather goods, clothing, jewelry, whatever.

Old Testament scholar Victor Matthews tells us that the city gate was both the busiest and the most vulnerable place in the community.[10] Not only did it control access for people moving in and out of the city, but it was the assembly area for important decisions the community leaders were called upon to make. As such, it was also the legal center of the town. It was at the city gate that the elders deliberated and then made pronouncements based on the law. It was there that important transactions were carried out, where court was convened, and where public announcements were given. When the prophet Amos called for repentance on the part of God's people, his complaint was (in part) based on the elders' practice of depriving the poor of justice in the courts at the gate (Amos 5:12).

Earlier, we met Ruth when she proposed marriage to the rich farmer Boaz. His response was that he would do what she had asked. Another relative had expressed some interest in marrying Ruth in order to obtain her mother-in-law's land. To follow through on his promise, Boaz "went up to the town gate and . . . took ten of the elders of the town" to sit in judgment regarding his deliberations with the other person. When Boaz called his rival's bluff, still at the city gate, he was then able to announce "to the elders and all the people, 'Today you are witnesses that I have bought from Naomi all the property of Elimelek, Kilion and Mahlon. I have also acquired Ruth the Moabite, Mahlon's widow, as my wife. . . . Today you are witnesses!' Then the elders and all those at the gate said, 'We are witnesses'" (Ruth 4:1–2, 9–11). That judicial process was another major function of the city gate.

Old Testament scholar Bruce Waltke tells us that the elders were the highest local authorities in the community. They represented the city's collective authority and power. Throughout the Old Testament, we see elders "sitting on the bench," tasked with applying God's law in ways that were fair for the people. Scholar Tremper Longman notes that the husband of our woman of strength could sit as an elder and make decisions affecting the entire community only because of her support. Her reputation enhanced his.

What if the husband had to give his time to clothing the family or feeding everyone in the household? What if earning a living wage as a farmer or tradesman took all of his time? Because he had a wife who had shouldered those responsibilities, he was able to serve as one of the highest authorities in the town. Proverbs 12:4 notes, "A wife of noble character is her husband's crown." Her work freed him to serve as a leader in the community. The chiasm makes that point.

Picture 4: A Woman Who Earns Her Money Selling Garments

"She makes linen garments and sells them, and supplies the merchants with sashes" (31:24). We've already noted that our woman of strength clothed her household, including the provision of warm clothes in winter. We've also noted that she was a businesswoman with an income that allowed her to invest in a vineyard. Now we learn the more precise nature of her income-producing work—creating and selling linen garments. What is clear is that she is active in a high-end market. Linen garments were generally considered luxury items. When Samson posed a riddle to some guests attending his marriage, the prize to be gained was "thirty linen garments" (Judges 14:12–13). Quality items of clothing were prized possessions, frequently passed down from one generation to the next.

Our *hayil* woman also supplied sashes to merchants. In Old Testament times, the basic dress for both men and women was a shirtlike garment (*kethoneth*) usually made of wool. Depending on need, status, or gender, these garments were worn either to the knee or to the ankle. Wealthier patrons often tied an ornamental sash around their waist. Sashes could be trimmed with blue threads or tassels and were made of linen, gauze, or silk. At times, these ornaments were a sign of a person's rank. When we think back to the care our woman of strength took in selecting her basic raw materials (the wool and flax of verse 13), it does not surprise us that she produced clothing that would sell well.

Picture 5: A Woman Clothed in Strength and Dignity

Our chiasm serves us well, reminding us that while our woman of strength may dress each morning in "fine linen and purple," what gives her *hayil* status is her strength and dignity. We've been aware of her strength, but now we learn that she is also "robed" in dignity. What is that about?

We're inching closer now to the climax of Proverbs 31. We often think of dignity in terms of honor or the esteem we receive from others who acknowledge our worth. We sometimes define it as self-respect that influences how we carry ourselves. Some scholars would settle for that understanding of the word. As one scholar put it, "Since clothing may display style and status, so her demeanor displays strength and honor."[11] I could imagine someone saying, "She carries herself well." Look at her. Watch her walk. You can see that she's an aristocratic person. She exudes self-confidence!

But perhaps a better way to think about this woman's dignity is that she works hard because she trusts the Lord. Does that sound like a contradiction in terms? Working hard could sound as if it's all about my efforts. Trusting God could imply that it's all about God's efforts; He's taking care of me, so I can sit back and let that happen. But our *hayil* woman understands that she is called to partner with God. She knows that all kinds of bad things can happen—droughts, floods, sickness, poor crops. So she works hard to protect her household against such losses. At the same time, she partners with God, putting her trust in Him.

We can be "dignified" on the basis of our accomplishments, but that can be short-lived. The dignity described in Proverbs 31 comes from a different reality. When we begin to grasp that we are created in God's image (Genesis 1:27), and as such we've been given the vocation of mirroring God's values in a broken world, it does something to our spine. We stand up taller (at least inside). We have a deeper dignity because we understand that we're in a partnership with the living God.

Picture 6: A Woman Able to Laugh

"When it snows, she has no fear for her household. . . . She can laugh at the days to come" (Proverbs 31:21, 25). Our chiasm is complete as our woman of strength contemplates her accomplishments on behalf of her household. Let it snow! She has seen to it that everyone in the house has warm clothing. Already in verse 14 she had made sure that they had enough to eat. Now, as she looks to the future, she can smile.

An Impossible Ideal, or A Model for Us Today?

It's easy to look at all that this woman has accomplished and simply write her off as a workaholic. We might shake our heads and declare her to be obsessive-compulsive. Or we might conclude that what she did two thousand years ago isn't possible for women today. We don't want the pressure to do the impossible. Where's the fun in that?

I see three things that keep me from simply dismissing this woman as an impossible model. First, I can see value in being trustworthy, diligent, dependable, forward-thinking, and generous. When I think about the opposite of each of these characteristics, I pull back: *Why would I want to be known as someone who is untrustworthy, lazy, undependable, or miserly?* The book of Proverbs demonstrates the consequences we suffer if we think we can get away with any of these opposites. They just don't pay! When we're not trustworthy, our relationships suffer. People can't count on us. We might think that gripping our finances tightly hurts no one, but it does hurt us. As noted in the previous chapter, we can easily become miserly when we fail to temper our shrewdness with generosity. Because I applaud the values that govern this woman's use of her time, I can't just write her off as an impossible model.

Second, this final poem in the book of Proverbs is a summary of the wisdom of the book as a whole. I've been appalled when some commentators have treated the final twenty-two verses of this book as irrelevant. Some have even concluded that it was tacked on long after the proverbs were assembled.

These verses were anything but an add-on, and good scholars are quick to affirm the importance of this chapter as a digest of the book's contents in a memorable acrostic form, designed to be memorized.

It may come as a surprise to some that the author chose to use a woman's work and world to give us this succinct summation of the main themes covered in the various proverbs. It's here that we recall that the first poem in Proverbs 31 (31:1–9) was addressed to King Lemuel with advice worthy of a ruler. Bruce Waltke helps us see that *all* of Proverbs 31 is addressed to King Lemuel, advising him about choices he faces. In the first poem he is reminded that the wrong kind of woman can ruin him (31:3) and that an addiction to alcohol can destroy his responsibility to the poor and needy (31:4–7). Then in the second poem (31:10–31), he is given a picture of a woman he can trust and depend on in every way. As a woman, I might imagine other reasons why the poet used a woman to depict the wisdom of the book of Proverbs. But when I see how closely the two poems are linked, I begin to understand that only a woman of strength could be a worthy consort to a civic leader or a king.

Third, we may be overwhelmed by a single reading of this passage, wondering how any human being could accomplish so much. But it's essential to see that the many activities of our woman of strength were not all carried out in the same way or on the same day! When I look back over my life, I see that being diligent, for example, looked different at different times. In school, I benefited when I was diligent in my studies. During my years with children in the home, my diligence focused on meeting their needs. When we had an empty nest, the need for diligence shifted to my work in teaching the Scriptures in various ways and places. Being generous also changes with changing circumstances. Sometimes we have funds that can be given to God's causes. Other times, our generosity shows up in the time we give to hurting people. How we use our time and our other resources necessarily varies according to needs, opportunities, and seasons of life.

What matters is that we respond in wise ways to each day's challenges. When wisdom guides our values and work, we will use our time to accomplish all that really needs to be done. That includes *not* squandering our time on things that really don't need our attention. Someone might think that the five minutes I spend each morning making our bed is a silly use of time, and if it took an hour rather than five minutes, I would probably agree. So we each make decisions about how we use our time. Those decisions will vary from one person to another. What counts is whether or not we practice being trustworthy or dependable or diligent or generous. The psalmist put it this way: "Teach us to number our days, that we may gain a heart of wisdom" (Psalm 90:12). If we want a heart of wisdom, we'll recognize that every day we make choices about the use of our time and resources. "Numbering our days" is about the decisions we make on the use of our time as women of strength. We can't do everything. But we can choose to give ourselves to the tasks that mark us as the women of strength we'd like to be.

Lord, I have to remind myself that this woman of strength didn't do everything on her bucket list in the same day or week. Still, I can be overwhelmed by all of her activities and accomplishments. Help me discern what is right for me to do, one day and one moment at a time. Remind me of things I may be neglecting unnecessarily. I really do want to live my life wisely. But I need help in knowing what that looks like in this season of my life. Amen.

For Reflection or Discussion

1. What do you consider to be the hardest choices you have to make from day-to-day?

2. When you face multiple demands on your time, what helps you figure out how to prioritize them?

3. What role might prayer or meditation play in deciding on any course of action?

4. Who are the people you turn to for help with decisions about your many responsibilities?

9

A Woman of Strength
Controls Her Tongue

She speaks with wisdom,
and faithful instruction is on her tongue.

Proverbs 31:26

Over the years, most of us have listened to a lot of people talk. While we probably haven't consciously thought about what we liked or disliked in what we've heard, we do have preferences. I'm rather deliberate when I speak, so I could never be a newscaster on television! They have to deliver the news at a very quick clip. Because I do speak a bit more slowly, I prefer others to speak to me in that way as well. If they speak rapidly, I may miss key points because I don't have time to process what I'm hearing. That's definitely a disadvantage, especially when I'm being given directions to get someplace. Recently, I needed help with creating a slide presentation, but within thirty seconds I was completely lost and I insisted that my tutor slow down and let me take notes on the process.

In addition to preferences about *how* we're spoken to, most of us also have preferences about *what* we like to hear. Because of the way I grew up, speech laced with profanity is like a fingernail on an old-fashioned blackboard: it sends shivers down my spine. But I can stand that better than someone who's "smarting off"—deliberately saying rude or irritating things. Some people are downright nasty. They'd fall over in a faint before they'd say something kind. While I feel sorry for them that they live in such a negative and destructive mental world, I avoid them when I can.

So what *do* I like to hear? I like to hear things that make me laugh. And I like to hear things that encourage me. I don't like downers. I also like to hear things about myself—things that prompt me to do even better. In the news broadcasts on television, in the midst of all the bad news, I like to hear that values I hold have been honored in some way. In church, I like being reminded of God's love and care instead of a negative rant about the culture or the politics of the day. In short, I want to hear things that give me the understanding and the energy to do what is good and right. But when I turn to Proverbs 31:26 and I read about a woman who always "speaks with wisdom, and faithful instruction is on her tongue," I tend to back away from her. She sounds too good to be true. I'm reasonably sure I do not measure up, and I'm certain I would not survive a comparison to such a paragon. But here I go prejudging her. I at least owe her the courtesy of hearing her out.

Listening to a *Hayil* Woman When She Speaks

"She speaks with wisdom, and faithful instruction is on her tongue" (Proverbs 31:26). The first thing to note is that this translation from the NIV is somewhat misleading. Scholar Bruce Waltke's more accurate translation from the Hebrew text is, "Her mouth she opens with wisdom, and loving teaching is on her tongue."[12] Both the New American Standard Bible and the New Revised Standard Version translate the Hebrew text this way: "She opens her mouth in [or "with"] wisdom, and the teaching of kindness is on her tongue." The Common English Bible also notes that "kindly teaching is on her tongue," whereas the New King James reads, "And on her tongue is the law of kindness." Rather than being about "faithful instruction" (as the NIV puts it), in addition to speaking with wisdom, her speech is controlled in some way by kindness.

Translation issues aside, we must conclude that when she speaks, this woman is both wise and kind. It's possible to be wise—to have a form of earthy wisdom—and yet speak in a nasty way. It's also possible to speak kindly but talk nonsense. This woman says wise things and she says them kindly. What a combination!

Up to this point in Proverbs 31, we've met a woman who seems to be tireless in all of her enterprises. We've followed her as she shopped for the best wool and flax, and we've watched her turn those raw materials into clothing for her household and high-end garments she sells to merchants. We've noted her attention to keeping good food on the table for everyone under her roof, even as she scouted for suitable land she could turn into a profitable vineyard. And we've been just a bit surprised that much of her work was done so she could use her earnings to help needy folks. Now, with verse 26, we've moved from examining her activities and accomplishments to how she speaks to everyone around her. That's important to know, but what we learn can also take us by surprise.

Given what we already know about this woman, she might seem more than a bit beyond what ordinary people accomplish day-to-day. She appears to be perpetually in motion. Then there are the references in Proverbs 31 that we didn't even touch. In verse 13, we're told that "she gets up before dawn" to see to breakfast for her household. Then in verse 18, we learn that "her lamp burns late into the night." (Some translations tell us that her lamp never goes out at night.) We're tempted to ask whether she ever gets a good night's sleep. We know that when we're tired, that affects how we speak to others around us. So we could assume that when she talks, she's curt or sharp-tongued as she moves through each day. If so, it may take us completely by surprise to learn in verse 26 that her speech is marked by wisdom and kindness.

Her Speech Reveals Her Wisdom

While most scholars see our woman of strength as a real person, not as a literary creation or archetype, her story also serves as a summary of all of the wisdom in the book of Proverbs. When we watch her, we are seeing wisdom enacted in real life. How she speaks helps us understand why the book of Proverbs has a lot to say about the difference between a wise or a foolish use of words. Here are a few examples:

- "The heart of the righteous weighs its answers, but the mouth of the wicked gushes evil" (15:28). There is wisdom in thinking before we speak!
- "To answer before listening—that is folly and shame" (18:13). Again, we are wise when we listen before responding.
- "Sin is not ended by multiplying words, but the prudent hold their tongues" (10:19). We're cautioned about talking too much. When it comes to words, less is almost always more.
- "The lips of fools bring them strife, and their mouths invite a beating. The mouths of fools are their undoing, and their lips are a snare to their very lives" (18:6–7). Words literally have the power of life and death!

Okay, there is wisdom in controlling our speech. It might keep us from getting into regrettable, even hurtful situations. In contrast to the dangers of foolish chatter, the book of Proverbs also identifies some important benefits of wise speech:

- "A gentle answer turns away wrath, but a harsh word stirs up anger. The tongue of the wise adorns knowledge, but the mouth of the fool gushes folly. . . . The soothing tongue is a tree of life, but a perverse tongue crushes the spirit" (15:1–2, 4). Gentle answers, gentle words: what a difference they can make when tempers flare.

- "The words of the reckless pierce like swords, but the tongue of the wise brings healing" (12:18). Most of us know the pain of cutting remarks, but how we respond to those cutting remarks can make a great difference.

Let me step away from our *hayil* woman for a moment to look at a larger piece of the Bible. Five books in the middle of the Old Testament together are labeled "Wisdom Literature." These are Job, Psalms, Proverbs, Ecclesiastes, and the Song of Songs. These five books give us many pictures of wisdom in action. For example, the book of Job is a picture of an extended conversation among Job and three "friends" who've come to console him when he loses his family, his wealth, and his health. The friends pepper him with reasoning (a kind of wisdom) that Job counters with a wisdom that God approves. The picture of Job, sitting by the fire scraping his sores with a piece of broken pottery, shows us his efforts to fend off a wisdom he rejects.

The picture in the Song of Songs is that of a man and woman, very much in love, exploring their sexual relationship salted with wisdom. In contrast, the picture in Ecclesiastes is one of an old king reflecting on what he had thought was wise in his youth and coming to understand what really matters in his mature years. The Psalms, of course, repeatedly show God's wisdom at work in supporting folks through every kind of difficulty.

That brings us to the book of Proverbs, which opens with the picture of Lady Wisdom in the town square, calling to young men to rethink their lives and choose to live wisely, not foolishly. Then the book of Proverbs concludes with a living picture of that wisdom in the life of our *hayil* woman. We've been watching her in action. Now we listen to her. What we hear is that her words are wise. She knows that "Whoever is patient has great understanding, but one who is quick-tempered displays folly" (Proverbs 14:29).

The bottom line is simply that "the tongue has the power of life and death" (18:21). So we're urged to "Walk with the wise and become wise," because the alternative is that "a companion of fools suffers harm" (13:20). When we are wise, "from a wise mind comes wise speech; the words of the wise are persuasive" (16:23 NLT). That is a powerful result we can enjoy when we are wise.

But, as we noted previously, in addition to her wisdom, the *hayil* woman of strength also gives instruction with kindness. She's wise enough not to clobber people over the head when they need guidance or correction.

Her Speech Reveals Her Kindness

This woman's kind speech is wrapped up in a Hebrew word whose meaning may be hard to nail down in English. It's the Hebrew word *hesed*. It's used more than eighty times in the Old Testament. Sometimes it means "goodness" or "a good deed," but more often it is translated as "kindness," "loyalty," "favor," or "unfailing love." So when we see the word "loyalty" in the Bible, it may be a translation of *hesed*. For example, in 2 Samuel 3, the context is the war between King Saul's armies and the followers of David (who had been anointed as king over Judah). Abner, Saul's commander-in-chief, has been loyal (*hesed*) to Saul but is now switching sides. A *hesed* kind of loyalty is not casual allegiance, such as a mild preference for one sporting team over another. It is an all-out and all-encompassing kind of loyalty. In contemporary terms, an Abner-like reversal would mean more than simply switching my vote from one candidate to his or her opponent; it would include dropping all other responsibilities and working tirelessly for the candidate I now support. A *hesed* kind of loyalty goes the limit. That's the kind of loyalty for which Abner was known.

A few times in the Old Testament, *hesed* is translated as "favor." Recall the story of Esther. King Xerxes decided to replace the queen, Vashti, when she refused to show off her beauty to his drunken friends. Rather than simply choosing another woman from the king's harem, Xerxes called for a search to find a new, stunningly beautiful woman—some gorgeous body he could show off as his next queen.

> When the king's order and edict had been proclaimed, many young women were brought to the citadel of Susa and put under the care of Hegai. Esther also was taken to the king's palace and entrusted to Hegai, who had charge of the harem. She pleased him and won his favor [*hesed*]. (Esther 2:8–9)

Such favor went beyond merely choosing Esther as the most likely candidate to succeed Vashti as queen. Hegai's favor toward Esther meant that he "immediately provided her with her beauty treatments and special food. He assigned to her seven female attendants selected from the king's palace and moved her and her attendants into the best place in the harem" (2:9). Hegai's favor was a kindness that went beyond what any other women were given. So *hesed* includes favor as one of its meanings.

But *hesed* is most often translated as "kindness." That brings us a bit closer to the radical meaning of this Hebrew word, but we're still not fully grasping its significance. Old Testament scholar Bruce Waltke notes that the word has a depth for which there is no English equivalent. He describes it as a person's willingness to reach out and help someone in need without any obligation to do so. The help is given freely, and somehow in the process it reflects kindness, mercy, love, and loyalty all rolled into one. We find the clearest example of this word when we listen to Isaiah reporting God's commitment to his people: "'Though the mountains be shaken and the hills be removed, yet my unfailing love [*hesed*] for you will not be shaken nor my covenant of peace be removed,' says the LORD who has compassion on you" (Isaiah 54:10). That picture of God's heart for His people comes closest to the meaning of this rich Hebrew word—it is "unfailing love."

When God's people had been in exile for seventy years, a remnant returned to the land of Israel under Nehemiah's leadership and prayed, "Our ancestors became arrogant and stiff-necked, and they did not obey your commands. They refused to listen and failed to remember the miracles you performed among them. . . . But you are a forgiving God, gracious and compassionate, slow to anger and abounding in love. Therefore you did not desert them" (Nehemiah 9:16–17). Note those adjectives: forgiving, gracious, compassionate, slow to anger, abounding in love. Put them all together into one and you get a sense of the scope of *hesed*. We read that, and it's almost beyond our comprehension that God should be so patient with our waywardness. Yet, the testimony of the Bible is that God loves us with that kind of unfailing love.

The Bible tells us that God is "the blessed and only Ruler,

the King of kings and Lord of lords, who alone is immortal and who lives in unapproachable light, whom no one has seen or can see" (1 Timothy 6:15–16). That's power beyond any human power. It's the power that created all that is. It's a terrifying power! But that God is also the God who loves us with unfailing love. "For I am convinced," writes the apostle Paul, "that neither death nor life, neither angels or demons, neither the present nor the future, nor any powers, neither height nor depth, nor anything else in all creation will be able to separate us from the love of God that is in Christ Jesus our Lord" (Romans 8:38–39). This is what *hesed* kindness looks like. It is a passionate and unfailing love at work for us in all our neediness.

This gives us the larger context we need to understand what it means that our *hayil* woman of strength speaks with *hesed*. Think back to all we've learned about this woman of strength. She most likely had daily conversations with her husband, with family members, and also with her servant girls, with the person selling her a field, and then with all of the people she had to hire to remove rocks and stones from that field before she could turn it into a vineyard. In addition, she had conversations with the laborers who built the stone walls and tower that her vineyard needed. Of course, she talked with the merchants selling her wool, flax, and food for the family. And she talked with the other merchants who purchased the linen garments and sashes she made as part of her business. And it's likely that she talked with some of the poor and needy who benefited from her generosity. In short, over the course of any day or week, this woman had many opportunities to speak sharply or cuttingly—but she didn't. Instead, "on her tongue is the law of kindness [*hesed*]" (Proverbs 31:26 NKJV).

Bible translators differ in their interpretation of what it means that "*hesed* teaching is on her tongue." Some believe she is teaching the folks in her household to be kind. For example, the New Revised Standard translation is that "the teaching of kindness is on her tongue." Other translators simply see the phrase as meaning that when she teaches wisdom to her household, she does so kindly.

Imagine a woman ruled by a soft way of speaking, guided by a *hesed* sort of kindness. In Shakespeare's tragic play *King Lear,* the king has three daughters—two who undermine his reign by sweet words but cruel acts, and one, Cordelia, who devotedly loves and supports her aging father. When the oldest daughter engineers Cordelia's death, Shakespeare puts these words of reminiscence into the mouth of the king as he mourns the tragic loss of his beloved daughter: "Her voice was ever soft, gentle, and low—an excellent thing in woman."[13] I was forced to learn that line in high school, but I did not appreciate the inference that women had requirements that did not also apply to men. It seemed to me that men should also be governed by soft, gentle speech. But setting gender aside, I've come to recognize the value of wise words soaked in *hesed.*

The Proverbs writer notes that, "Wisdom reposes in the heart of the discerning and even among fools she lets herself be known" (14:33). That proverb brings to mind a remarkably wise woman named Abigail who was married to a fool named Nabal. We find their story in 1 Samuel 25:2–42.

A *Hayil* Woman Whose Wise Words Averted Tragedy

Nabal was wealthy, owning three thousand sheep and one thousand goats tended in unfenced land. For a year, David and his band had protected Nabal's shepherds from marauders. The grateful shepherds reported to Nabal that David's men "were like a wall of protection to us and the sheep" (1 Samuel 25:16). At sheep-shearing time, David's envoys presented themselves to Nabal, asking for some payment, which Nabal refused to give them. Incensed, David armed four hundred of his men and set out for the fool's ranch, determined to destroy Nabal and all he had.

Meanwhile, a servant privy to the situation told Nabal's wise wife, Abigail, what was about to happen. She quickly set about assembling a large quantity of food and drink as a gift to David, then stealthily set off on her donkey to intercept David and his men. Riding through a mountain ravine, she saw David and his band ahead just as David groused, "It's been useless—all my watching over this fellow's property in the wilderness so that nothing of his was missing. He has paid me back evil for good. May God deal with David, be it ever so severely, if by morning I leave alive one male of all who belong to him!" (25:21–22).

Slipping off her donkey, Abigail bowed to the ground, apologized for her husband, and presented David with all that she had brought for him. Listen to how wisely and kindly she spoke to her husband's enemy: "As surely as the LORD your God lives and as you live, since the LORD has kept you from bloodshed and from avenging yourself with your own hands, may your enemies and all who are intent on harming my lord be like Nabal. And let this gift, which your servant has brought to my lord, be given to the men who follow you" (25:26–27).

Wise words kindly spoken, and a disaster was averted.

David accepted her gifts of food, replying to her, "Praise be to the LORD, the God of Israel, who has sent you today to meet me. May you be blessed for your good judgment and for keeping me from bloodshed this day and from avenging myself with my own hands. . . . If you had not come quickly to meet me, not one male belonging to Nabal would have been left alive by daybreak" (25:32–34).

Of course, Abigail still had to deal with Nabal on her return home. In her absence, he had thrown a big party and was totally drunk. Wisely, she waited until he was sober to tell him what she had done. What would he think or do when he learned of the danger to his life she had averted? Shout for joy? Lash out in anger? Neither, as it turned out. As he heard her speak, he had a stroke and died ten days later.

Do you like happily-ever-after endings? If so, you might like to know that as soon as David heard that Nabal was dead, he wasted no time in proposing marriage to Abigail. That woman's wise words and gentle spirit had impressed him to the point that he wanted Abigail as his wife. Abigail's response? The text tells us she "quickly got on a donkey and, attended by her five female attendants, went with David's messengers, and became his wife" (25:42).

As you probably already know, David later did become king over all Israel and lived in a palace in Jerusalem. But as time went by, he also acquired seven other wives, so Abigail was one among eight royal spouses. We hear nothing further about her. But we remember her for her wisdom and her kindness. Like the Proverbs 31 woman of strength, when Abigail spoke, her words were wise, and she gave instruction with kindness. She knew what we sometimes forget—that, "Gracious words are a honeycomb, sweet to the soul and healing to the bones" (Proverbs 16:24).

Lord, if there's anything I struggle with, it's that my words are not always spoken wisely and kindly. I know better, but I need your help to set a guard over my mouth. I understand the wisdom of maintaining a gentle spirit that would keep me from sharp words that bite and hurt. Yet, it's tempting at times to use those sharp words in hurtful ways. Please give me the strength I need to speak wisely and kindly. Amen.

For Reflection or Discussion

1. As you think about the Proverbs 31 woman of strength, what stands out as the most difficult trait to emulate?

2. What do you think is the easiest trait to emulate?

3. How important do you think it is that we always speak wisely and kindly?

4. What makes speaking wisely and kindly difficult for you at times?

10

A Woman of Strength
Blesses Her Household

She watches over the affairs of her household
and does not eat the bread of idleness.
Her children arise and call her blessed;
her husband also, and he praises her:
"Many women do noble things,
but you surpass them all."

Proverbs 31:27–29

It's nice to be praised. And when that praise is deserved, it's even nicer. In contrast, few things are more frustrating than working hard and accomplishing something significant, only to have no one say a good word about what we've done (or worse, to steal the credit for our work). It's not that we've accomplished something just for praise. But at the same time, we're encouraged to keep on track when our work is appreciated.

Over the years, I've held a number of jobs. When my work was praised, it caused me to redouble my efforts to accomplish even more for my employers. But I recall with some pain a job in which the praise I deserved was not given. In fact, my necessary work was discounted. When it was appropriate, I gave notice that I would leave that job four months later. I then created a calendar for those four months and at the end of each day's work, I took great satisfaction in making a heavy black **X** across that day's date, noting those days remaining before I could leave that employ. Was I being petty? Probably. But I do know the pain of having no praise when it was deserved versus the value of praise in motivating me to keep up my good work.

There's something about praise that energizes us. It spurs us on. Praise can motivate us to watch how we speak as well as how we act. It can enable us to go the second mile in our care of our responsibilities. We've watched our *hayil* woman prove her trustworthiness in her care for her family, in her successful business ventures, and in the many ways her diligence benefited her husband's role as a community leader. Now we learn that her family recognizes her diligence and praises her for it. Her children call her blessed. Her husband notes, "Many women do noble things, but you surpass them all." High praise indeed!

What Is This "Bread of Idleness"?

Note the summarizing statement that generates such praise: "She watches over the affairs of her household and does not eat the bread of idleness" (Proverbs 31:27). We've already seen her vigilance in assuring warm clothing for her household, then food, often brought "from afar" to nourish hungry stomachs. Then we've seen her step outside the house to explore the possibility of creating a productive vineyard. We've watched her pace that empty field, measuring it for potential productivity before purchasing it. Then we've seen it encircled by a rock wall and protected by a watchtower in its midst. We've learned that she could finance all of that construction because she had a productive business making and selling linen garments to merchants. But we've also watched her spin thread and weave sashes so she could give generously to others in need. We've been told that her industry benefited her husband, releasing him from domestic responsibilities so he could serve as a leader in their town. We don't doubt the writer of this poem when we're told that "she watches over the affairs of her household." That's obvious. And it explains the reason for the praise she receives from her children and her husband.

The text actually tells us that she keeps a sharp, vigilant lookout over everything touching her household. She stays on top of things. She maintains order in the household. The Hebrew verb implies that she deals promptly with anything that disrupts her orderly arrangement of things. In other words, she stays ahead of disaster so she isn't rushing from one catastrophe to another. This watchfulness is not an on-again-off-again practice. It's linked to the last part of the sentence: "and does not eat the bread of idleness."

There can be a downside to not eating the bread of idleness. So it was important for me to learn in our previous chapter that our woman of strength always spoke wisely and kindly. If I had first learned that she did not eat the bread of idleness, I would probably have assumed that she was so constantly on top of everything in the house that her voice was strident as she barked out commands about "wiping your feet" or "rinse that glass and put it in the dishwasher—don't leave it in the sink." Everyone else in the house would be held hostage to her perfectionism. When we've been around such housekeepers, we rarely relax, afraid that we will inadvertently mess things up. But in some wonderful way, a woman of strength can retain a warm, caring relationship to everyone in the family while still maintaining the household efficiently.

What Do We Know About Those Who Do Eat the Bread of Idleness?

The book of Proverbs was assembled "for gaining wisdom and instruction; for understanding words of insight; for receiving instruction in prudent behavior, doing what is right and just and fair" (1:2–3). The book then ends with the *hayil* woman showing us what that kind of disciplined and successful life looks like. But between Proverbs 1 and 31 we are introduced to those who *do* "eat the bread of idleness." The contrast between disciplined, successful folks and those munching on the bread of idleness is clear: "The way of the sluggard is blocked with thorns, but the path of the upright is a highway" (15:19). Or, "Lazy hands make for poverty, but diligent hands bring wealth" (10:4).

So people eating the bread of idleness will face unnecessary obstacles, possible poverty, and certainly the irritation of those who depend on them. So the writer gives such folks some advice: "Go to the ant, you sluggard; consider its ways and be wise! It has no commander, no overseer or ruler, yet it stores its provisions in summer and gathers its food at harvest" (6:6–8). No one is standing over those ants, forcing them to labor hard all summer. They do it freely because they know that winter will come and they need to stock up against that time. That's a suitable model for us.

At the risk of being redundant, the proverbs come back again and again to the consequences for those who eat the bread of idleness. For example, the writer asks the sluggard, "How long will you lie there? When will you get up from your sleep? . . . Poverty will come on you like a thief and scarcity like an armed man" (6:9–11). Another proverb predicts that "the shiftless go hungry" (19:15). In sum, "The craving of a sluggard will be the death of him, because his hands refuse to work" (21:25).

Writers of the proverbs sometimes employed vivid pictures describing the consequences of being a lazy person. For example, "I went past the field of a sluggard, past the vineyard of someone who has no sense; thorns had come up everywhere, the ground was covered with weeds, and the stone wall was in ruins. I applied my heart to what I observed and learned a lesson from what I saw: A little sleep, a little slumber, a little folding of the hands to rest" followed by the pounce of poverty (24:30–33). That's not a nice prospect! Another vivid picture is about someone too lazy to work who tells everyone, "There's a lion on the road, a fierce lion roaming the streets!" (26:13). This person will do anything—even dreaming up something as preposterous as a lion in the streets—to keep from doing any work.

But in making a case for not "eating the bread of idleness," our woman of strength is not someone who stays busy just to be busy. We note that her busyness is focused. Since we first met her in verse 11, we've watched her making sure that everyone under her roof had adequate food and clothing, then that her business prospered, enabling her to be generous to the poor and needy. And we've noted that she also is not a busybody, someone eager for gossip. Instead, "When she speaks, her words are wise, and she gives instructions with kindness" (31:26 NLT). In short, her activities and her words are purposeful. She's not busy just to keep busy.

The Complexity of Watching Over a Household

Have you ever stopped to think about the way in which a household is a complex operation with many moving parts? Every household has people in it, and the more people, the more possibilities for clashes in needs, in schedules, in demands for service or responses to those demands. In addition, every household has a wide range of tasks that must be attended to if folks are to eat or sleep or work or play. Those tasks include laundry and cleaning and cooking and planning for grocery shopping and car maintenance and assuring that all bills are paid on time, and so on. And that's just barely scratching the surface.

Another layer of moving parts in any household touches not just physical needs but also emotional and spiritual needs. Who needs encouragement? Who needs a gentle correction? Who needs instruction—teaching covering a wide range of needs? Some may need teaching about personal hygiene or habits. Others may need teaching about kinder approaches in interactions. Still others may need encouragement in following God more nearly. And most need help in appreciating the needs of everyone else in the household. As a result, most of us are impressed when our woman of strength "always speaks kindly." If family members have any understanding of all of these moving parts comprising any home, they will praise the person who holds it all together peaceably. No wonder this woman's children rise up and call her blessed.

Her Children Praise Our Woman of Strength

The word *blessed* is one of those nice-sounding words with religious overtones. We bump into it often throughout the Bible. While the English word can be used to translate several Hebrew words, *ashar*—the Hebrew word used and translated here as "blessed"—frequently means "to declare happy." It's as if the kids in the family look up and say, "Hey, Mom, great job! Be happy! Because of you, things keep turning out so well!" This Hebrew word occurs only four times in the Old Testament. To get a better sense of its meaning, let's look at the other three places where it is used.

The first use of *ashar* is in Genesis. When Leah, Jacob's unloved first wife, could no longer get pregnant, she gave her servant Zilpah to Jacob, hoping that he would impregnate her. When Zilpah conceived and gave birth, the baby became Leah's. She then named the infant Asher, exclaiming, "What joy [*ashar*] is mine! Now the other women will celebrate with me!" (30:13 NLT). Here, the word describes the pleasure we feel when things turn out well.

We next come upon *ashar* in Psalm 72:17, where it appears to have a different sense. But first, a few words about the entire psalm. This psalm closes with the words, "This concludes the prayers of David son of Jesse" (72:20). Throughout the psalm, David, now an old man, prays for his son, Solomon, who is ascending the throne as ruler over prosperous Israel. David begins this final prayer with these words: "Give your love of justice to the king, O God, and righteousness to the king's son. Help him judge your people in the right way; let the poor always be treated fairly. . . . Help him to defend the poor, to rescue the children of the needy, and to crush their oppressors" (72:1–2, 4 NLT). It is for a king with these concerns that David then prays, "May the king's name endure forever; may it continue as long as the sun shines. May all nations be blessed [*ashar*] through him and bring him praise" (72:17 NLT). This blessing on the nations isn't just about being "happy." It's much closer to the Hebrew word *shalom*, which is often translated as peace but has a much richer meaning. David's prayer is that these nations will experience not just peace, but wholeness or universal flourishing.

The final use of *ashar* is in Malachi, the last book in the Old Testament. The people of God, those who have returned from exile in Persia, are once again established and comfortable in their historic land. But the priesthood is corrupt, and many priests have forsaken the ancient covenant God had made with them. The prophet Malachi's task is to call them back. God's word to them is that they are under a curse for cheating God of the tithes and offerings due him. The promise is that if they return to the covenant and its obligations, the Lord of Heaven's Armies "will open the windows of heaven for you" (3:10 NLT). Crops will be abundant and guarded from insects and diseases. Grapes won't fall from the vine before they are ripe. "'Then all nations will call you blessed [ashar], for your land will be such a delight,' says the Lord of Heaven's Armies" (3:12 NLT). Again, the sense of blessedness appears closer to God's *shalom* than simply to happiness.

So we see that *ashar* can be translated as "happy" or "joy," but it also has the deeper sense of blessedness, even of *shalom*, the blessing of wholeness, of flourishing, of delight. In that sense, it is also appropriate to the family. As the children of the *hayil* woman rise up and call her blessed, that blessing may include not just our woman of strength but also the flourishing of the entire household under her watchfulness.

Translators of *ashar* give us two significantly different interpretations of that Hebrew word in Proverbs 31:28. Some translators understand the word to mean that her children take note of her happiness and rejoice in it. Other translators understand this text to mean that her children "stand and bless her." In other words, the way they are turning out is a source of joy or happiness for her. Whether the text states that the children of our *hayil* woman rejoice in her happiness or that they make her happy, the bottom line is that parents are happy when their children stand up and praise them!

We are grateful when our children can see the unnumbered times when we've set aside our own agenda in order to sit with them, work with them, cry with them, laugh with them, or go to bat for them. The kids in Proverbs 31:28 remind us that they see a parent's unceasing care for them and give praise where praise is due.

Her Husband Praises Our Woman of Strength

We then read the praise given our *hayil* woman by her husband: "Many women do noble things, but you surpass them all" (Proverbs 31:29). This second poem of Proverbs 31 had begun with a valiant woman being so rare that she's "more precious than rubies" (31:10 NLT). Now the husband states that there are many valiant women in the world, but our *hayil* woman tops them all. It's encouraging that our *hayil* woman is not unique, the one-and-only valiant woman around. That leaves open the possibility that other women can qualify to be such a woman! If we take this poem seriously, we can all capture and then live out its wisdom. So this isn't a contest to win the "most valiant wife" award. There's room for many winners. In fact, there are no losers when a woman chooses to become a woman of strength.

As we near the end of this poem climaxing the book of Proverbs, let's step back into the poem to see what the proud husband saw that drew such praise from him. He understood the extraordinary blessing of a wife who was trustworthy (31:11). She could be trusted to ensure clothing and food for the family (31:12–15). But she didn't stop there. She enabled him to serve as a leader in the community as she shouldered much of the responsibility to produce income. Her astute business dealings freed him to use his gifts in service of the city (31:16–18, 24). It was clear to him that her oversight of the entire household made for a happy and prosperous family (31:27–29). Blessed is the man who knows that he is blessed with such a consort! No wonder he concluded, "Many women do noble things, but you surpass them all" (31:29).

The Many Faces of Being a *Hayil* Woman

We all have differing lives and responsibilities. For some, our domain is the family. For others, it's the workplace. In some cases, it's a hospital with patients to care for, or tests to carry out, or surgeries to perform, or floors to sweep, or bedpans to empty. In other cases, it's a classroom with difficult students to teach, or working with children dealing with severe disabilities, or with graduate students who think they own the world. In many cases, we deal with difficult colleagues or poor pay for the work we do, or with employers who vacillate about the praise we deserve. In every case, we are called to be diligent in our work and also careful in our relationships.

As *hayil* women, we also recognize God's concern for "the widow, the orphan, and the stranger in the land." We understand and accept God's call to be generous toward the poor and needy. And if we yearn to be known as a *hayil* person, we'll guard our tongue. Proverbs 10:31 reminds us that, "From the mouth of the righteous comes the fruit of wisdom, but a perverse tongue will be silenced."

We know what the proverbs tell us about lazy people, about those who fail to carry through on their responsibilities. In every case, if we are *hayil* people, we won't "eat the bread of idleness." At the same time, we won't neglect self-care. To do so is to risk losing the capacity to carry out our responsibilities.

We've come full circle: even as the children and the husband have praised our *hayil* woman, the book concludes by calling the entire community to recognize our woman's accomplishments and to reward her with the praise she deserves. I've sometimes traveled in circles in which folks had a skewed idea about praise, withholding it so that it wouldn't give the recipient "a big head." But the book of Proverbs ends with these words: "Let [the *hayil* woman's] deeds publicly declare her praise." It is at the city gates—the most public place in a community—that her works will bring her praise. The entire community is called to recognize and honor this woman's works.

The book of Proverbs has one caveat about praise: "Let someone else praise you, not your own mouth; an outsider, and not your own lips" (27:2). Sometimes politicians toot their own horn. Sometimes professional sports personalities or celebrities make sure we sing their praises. And sometimes even Christians are tempted to boast of their superiority. Our *hayil* woman did not need to praise the work of her hands, nor do we. If our work deserves recognition and praise, wisdom tells us to let others give it.

Sometimes the praise we receive from others helps us see the value in what we've accomplished. Often, we do what needs to be done without our actually thinking about it—we go to it on automatic pilot. But when someone else sees our work and praises it, we discover an added value we might otherwise have missed. Praise can be like a great dessert after a good meal. If we've done our best in handling our responsibilities, we can pick up our fork and enjoy that dessert—the praise our work deserves.

$\rule{2cm}{0pt}$

Lord, I have two requests. First, I tend to focus on what I fail to do rather than on what I do accomplish. I need to see that the work of my hands can deserve praise. But second, I know that when I'm focused on my work, my tongue can get sharp. I want to bring wisdom and kindness to my speech, but when I get busy, that sometimes gets lost. At the same time, Lord, I want my work to be done because it honors you and helps others, not because I want it to be praised. With your help, I want to get this sorted out in my head and in my heart. For that I need guidance from your Spirit. Amen.

For Reflection or Discussion

1. How do you feel about staying on top of all the moving parts in the work you do?

2. What are the most challenging tasks you're called on to do?

3. What has been your experience with praise?

4. In what ways do you see God's hand in the work you've been given to do?

A Woman of Strength
Lives for What Lasts

Charm is deceptive, and beauty is fleeting;
    but a woman who fears the LORD is to be praised.
Honor her for all that her hands have done,
    and let her works bring her praise at the city gate.

Proverbs 31:30–31

When I was a child, the only way I could think about God was with terror. Fear of the Lord kept me awake at night and worried by day. I grew up in a devout family and in a church with a strong emphasis on evangelism. But I had somehow concluded that being "right with God" was a tricky business, and I wasn't sure that I wouldn't end up in hell despite my prayers to the contrary. Reading the Bible, I kept bumping into verses that talked about "the fear of the Lord." Perhaps you have experienced that same fear of God. It has taken many years to get my mind around a different view of God, one in which "fear" does not mean terror.

When we come to the conclusion of this second poem in Proverbs 31, we face the importance of "the fear of the Lord," noting that such fear stands as a positive contrast to things that don't last—specifically, charm and beauty. To be clear, there is nothing inherently evil about charm, and beauty can be one of God's gifts. While both can become obsessions, displacing more important things in our lives, the contrast between them and the fear of the Lord is not a license to deny that charm and beauty have any value.

Church history, however, might give us a different idea. By the late second century, both charm and beauty were considered evils by which women trapped men sexually, turning them from the godliness demanded by Christian leaders. As I've noted elsewhere,[14] a Christian woman was responsible not only for her chastity but also for the chastity of men. In order to avoid exciting a man's imagination sexually, she had to cover herself from head to toe in dark, shapeless clothing so no part of her form was seen. For example, Tertullian (ca. AD 155–340) wrote long treatises on what women wore and how they acted. Clement of Alexandria (ca. AD 150–215) preached against any female clothing that revealed the female figure. Instead, he wanted women attending church to be entirely covered, including a veil over the face. Such teachings were late-second- and early-third-century issues, so we might argue that Christian doctrine has moved permanently beyond such draconian notions. But even to this day, some groups of Christians continue to downplay any ornamentation in clothing that might draw attention to a woman's physical beauty or charm. So how are we to think about charm or beauty? And how do they contrast with "the fear of the Lord"?

Deceptive and Fleeting

The Hebrew word *chen*, translated here as "charm," most often means *grace*. When the word is used about a person, it generally refers to a loveliness of form or a gracefulness. Various dictionaries define charm as a physical grace or an attractiveness that delights others. In other words, someone who has charm behaves in a pleasant way that makes people like him or her. We can have charm without being beautiful. People with charm are the kind of folks we want as neighbors or friends. We like doing business with them because they are polite and helpful. It's nice to be with people who are genuinely glad to meet us. We're pleased when we express an opinion and a charming person "gets it." We like ourselves more when we feel valued by such folks. Most of us know some wonderfully charming people who are genuine and worthy of our trust.

But this gracefulness can at times be misleading. What we like in charming people might actually deceive us. They may be so agreeable that at times we assume they are with us when, in fact, they are not. It may simply be that they are so kind that they don't want to be disagreeable. On the other hand, folks with an agenda may use their charm to deceive us. With such pleasant folks, our defenses are often down. We don't filter comments or looks or actions that could alert us to a danger we have not imagined possible.

Charm can also be part of a strategy to fleece us. Particularly in any business dealings, we learn (sometimes too late) to accept a salesperson's charm simply as part of the deal, a way to persuade us to make a purchase we might not otherwise have made. If we conclude that we're the objects of a so-called charm offensive, our defenses immediately go up. Then we may be pleasantly surprised in those situations in which the charm is sincere and our friend has our best interests at heart. But at bottom, we know that charm has the potential to be deceptive.

What about beauty? Clearly, it doesn't last. But is it something we should not desire? Is it wrong for a woman or a man to take steps to enhance their potential beauty? When we turn to the Bible, we find not only the mention of various women deemed beautiful, but praise for their beauty. "Let the king be enthralled by your beauty," writes the psalmist, "honor him, for he is your lord" (Psalm 45:11). Those words come from a wedding song written for a choir. Nothing in this psalm puts a negative spin on physical beauty.

Or we can turn to the Song of Songs, a book of the Bible extolling the beloved's beauty: "You are beautiful, my darling, beautiful beyond words. Your eyes . . . your hair . . . your teeth . . . your smile . . . your lips . . . your cheeks . . . your neck . . . your breasts. . . . You are altogether beautiful, my darling, beautiful in every way" (Song of Songs 4:1–7 NLT). That may seem to be over-the-top, but the fact remains that the Bible sees beauty as God's gift. In fact, the Bible states that God "has made everything beautiful in its time" (Ecclesiastes 3:11).

God creates beauty. Whether we are awed by a magnificent garden, a starry sky or moonrise, or the sight of a stunning person, we know that God created beauty for our pleasure. God gave some folks such physical beauty that we take delight in looking at such a person. That God made everything beautiful for its own time pushes us to see that various times or circumstances may need something or someone beautiful.

Beauty often plays a role in God's plan. For example, if Esther had not been so beautiful, she would not have been chosen as Xerxes's new queen. Then the plot against the king's life would not have been disclosed to him by Esther's cousin. And the plot against the lives of all of the Jews in exile in

Persia would not have been overturned. Esther's beauty put her in a position to alert the king to the plot against his life and also to evil Haman's scheme for annihilating all of her people. It was her surpassing beauty that put her in the palace and allowed her to save her people from destruction.

It's true that beauty can be a problem for women who feel they lack it. We have only to turn to the story of Jacob's two wives, Leah and Rachel, to watch their rivalry play itself out in sad ways for many years. Uncle Laban, for whom Jacob was working, had two daughters: "Leah had weak eyes, but Rachel had a lovely figure and was beautiful" (Genesis 29:17). Jacob wanted to marry beautiful Rachel, the younger daughter. But Uncle Laban wanted to unload his older daughter first. In bed, after the marriage ceremony, Jacob expected the heavily veiled woman to be Rachel. What a shock when it turned out to be plain Leah! While the deception was Uncle Laban's plot, it was Leah who had to live with a man who despised her and longed for marriage to her sister.

So we see that beauty has its purpose, but it can also be the source of rivalry, jealousy, and insecurity. Furthermore, we acknowledge the truth of our text, "beauty is fleeting." If we live into old age, every time we look in a mirror, we see that whatever physical "beauty" we might have had in the past is now gone. So we're warned not to put our hope or our identity in something fleeting.

The Fear of the Lord

In contrast to the deceptive nature of charm and the fleeting nature of beauty, we then come to "the fear of the Lord." What did this mean to the *hayil* woman, and what could it mean for us today?

Because we bump into "the fear of the Lord" in many parts of the Bible, we know we can't avoid it. So we need to take time to grapple with its implications for our lives. In Deuteronomy we read, "For the LORD your God is God of gods and Lord of lords, the great God, mighty and awesome. . . . Fear the LORD your God and serve him. Hold fast to him. . . . He is the one you praise" (10:17, 20, 21). The apostle Paul sent this description in a letter to Timothy: "God, the blessed and only Ruler, the King of kings and Lord of lords, who alone is immortal and who lives in unapproachable light, whom no one has seen or can see. To him be honor and might forever" (1 Timothy 6:15–16). When Paul was in Athens, he came across an idol "to the unknown god." When asked by someone in the marketplace about such a god, he replied, "The God who made the world and everything in it is the Lord of heaven and earth and does not live in temples built by human hands. . . . He himself gives everyone life and breath and everything else" (Acts 17:24–25). In the final book of the New Testament, the Revelation, God speaks: "'I am the Alpha and the Omega,' says the Lord God, 'who is, and who was, and who is to come, the Almighty" (1:8). Such descriptions of God give us reason to fear the Lord. This is fear, as in being afraid.

But in the Bible, "the fear of the Lord" is not an emotion of terror; it is a fundamental awareness that we live in the presence of the living God. Once we accept that reality, it changes how we see life. And it also changes how we live our lives.

When we turn to the book of Proverbs, we discover some of the great benefits of "fearing the Lord." For starters, consider Proverbs 1:7: "The fear of the LORD is the beginning of knowledge." And we learn that "The fear of the LORD is the beginning of wisdom, and knowledge of the Holy One is understanding" (9:10). In some way, this fundamental awareness that we live in the presence of the living God opens our minds to knowledge and wisdom even as it expands our knowledge of God.

But what does it mean to "live in the presence of the living God"? It may help to think of it in human terms. Suppose I greatly admire an outstanding teacher. Then I'm given the opportunity to study under that teacher. I watch that teacher's actions. I listen carefully to what that teacher says. I grasp the values of that teacher and attempt to make those values my own. In short, I absorb all that I can living in the presence of that teacher so that my own knowledge and values are constantly being challenged, even upended.

But there is more. Not only do I absorb the values and knowledge that I admire in that teacher, I begin to spread those values and that knowledge to help others as I've been helped. And that takes me back to the opening chapter of the Bible. There, in the very first verse, is an explosive truth: God has unimaginable power, enough to bring into being the heavens and the earth. As I read what follows—the details of creation bringing life and order into this new creation—I come to verse 26 where I hear God talking:

> "Let us make mankind in our image, in our likeness, so that they may rule over the fish in the sea and the birds in the sky, over the livestock and all the wild animals, and over all the creatures that move along the ground."
>
> So God created mankind in his own image, in the image of God he created them, male and female he created them.
>
> God blessed them and said to them, "Be fruitful and increase in number; fill the earth and subdue it." (Genesis 1:26–28)

Let that soak in. We are not like God. Yet we were created in some way in God's own image. How can that be? Furthermore, we were created to "rule" over the rest of creation. We are stewards of God's new world. As one writer noted, we are

God's vice-regents, given responsibility to care for and manage all that has been put under us. How does that task relate to our creation in God's image?

Theologians have spilled huge amounts of ink while pontificating on what part of our being reflects the divine image. In the process, they mistake our innate personhood for our God-given task. As New Testament scholar N. T. Wright notes, we've been created to be "angled mirrors," reflecting God and His values into our broken world. This is our task. If you've ever driven in high mountains, you may have noticed that on narrow roads bordering a precipice, angled mirrors are often positioned so that the driver can see any oncoming traffic reflected at a blind curve. That's what God has called us to be. This God whom we fear has given us the responsibility to reflect God's values in our broken world.

"Living in the presence of the living God" ("fearing" God) gives us the opportunity to reflect God's values in an ungodly world. Our woman of strength did just that. She proved herself trustworthy, diligent, dependable, generous, kind, and determined to meet well all the needs of her household. Her "fear" of God was not fear as we think of it. She so lived in the presence of the living God that her life reflected the values of her Maker. That was her calling, and that is our calling today. Proverbs 14:27 tells us that "the fear of the LORD is a fountain of life." That was the experience of our woman of strength. It can be our experience today.

Meanwhile, Genesis 16 paints a slightly different picture of the fear of the Lord. In that picture we meet an Egyptian servant named Hagar. You may recall that Abraham and Sarah (*Abram* and *Sarai* at that time) could not have children. So, following the custom of the day, Sarah gave her servant Hagar to Abraham, hoping that Abraham would get her pregnant.

That worked, and during her pregnancy, Hagar taunted Sarah to the point that Sarah mistreated her harshly. At that point, Hagar deserted the family, fleeing into the desert.

As Hagar rested at a well on the road to Shur, God's angel appeared to her, asking, "Where have you come from and where are you going?" (16:8). To Hagar's reply, the angel then promised she would have a son whom she should name Ishmael, meaning, "God hears." From that encounter on, Hagar's name for God was, "You are the God who sees me" (16:13). The biblical text tells us that the well where Hagar rested was named *Beer Lahai Roi*, meaning "well of the Living One who sees me."

God sees me. There was a time when that thought terrified me. But I've since discovered that it's a thought that can transform the way I see life and my responsibilities in it. Obviously, the *hayil* woman in Proverbs 31 lived consistently with that reality. The awareness of going through each day in the presence of the living God guided all of her actions.

God of Power, Light, and Love

What is it about God that challenges what I might think when I'm driven by fear? In 1 John 1:5, we learn that "God is light; in him there is no darkness at all." When the light is good, we see things as they really are. John calls us to "walk in the light, as [God] is in the light" (1 John 1:7). John reminds us that in the light we can see ourselves clearly—and can deal with the things we think, say, or do that need to be acknowledged or confessed and then abandoned. This is one part of living with the "fear of the Lord." God's light shows us what we really are. Seeing ourselves—really seeing what and who we are— can cause us to fear God even more.

But that does not mean we need to fear God in the sense of

wrath or terror. God is not only light but also *love*. God's very essence is love. What difference does that make in our lives? The bright light of truth might scare us when it illumines who we really are. But when that light comes from God, whose very being is love, then we can endure the light.

The apostle John catalogs the ways in which God has acted out of love on our behalf. First, God shows us how much he loves us: "This is love: not that we loved God but that he loved us and sent his son as an atoning sacrifice for our sins" (1 John 4:10). Then the apostle reminds us, "No one has ever seen God; but if we love one another, God lives in us, and his love is made complete in us" (4:12).

Think of it: God lives in us, and furthermore, we live in God: "God is love. Whoever lives in love lives in God, and God in them," (4:16). Can you begin to imagine what that has the potential to release in each of us as we tap into God's presence in us? Most likely, it will release a strong desire to please God. Then, because God is holy, just, and good, it may release a strong desire to live our lives committed to what is holy, just, and good. For our *hayil* woman, it meant caring for the needs of her household, and also managing a successful business that enabled her husband to serve as a leader in the community.

For a dear friend, living in God's presence has meant giving her life to live in love for people in a country that kills or imprisons people who love and serve Jesus. For another dear friend, it has meant sinking all of her resources into the creation of a home for women leaving prison who need help to transition into productive living. For still another friend, it has meant earning an advanced degree in biblical studies, a field typically unfriendly to women in ministry, so she can speak and write.

So how are we to think about the fear of the Lord? We are to view all of life through the lens provided by the nature of

God as both light and love alive within us. The fear of the Lord motivates us to please God, not out of terror or fear of punishment, but because we love this God who sees us.

Those of us who have read (and reread!) the Narnia books might recall the moment in *The Lion, the Witch, and the Wardrobe* when Susan and Lucy have just learned that Aslan is a lion. Timidly, Lucy asked whether Aslan was safe, to which Mrs. Beaver replied:

> "If there's anyone who can appear before Aslan without their knees knocking, they're either braver than most or else silly."
>
> "Then he isn't safe?" said Lucy.
>
> "Safe?" said Mr. Beaver; "don't you hear what Mrs. Beaver tells you? Who said anything about safe? 'Course he isn't safe. But he's good. He's the King, I tell you."

Aslan, a metaphor for Christ, is not safe, but he's good. God is the "the blessed and only Ruler, the King of kings and Lord of lords, who alone is immortal and who lives in unapproachable light, whom no one has seen or can see" (1 Timothy 6:15–16). Reading that verse in fear alone, we might ask Lucy's question, "Is he safe"? The answer is that God is love: He loves us with a love that will not let us go.

"Charm is deceptive, and beauty is fleeting; but a woman who fears the LORD is to be praised" (Proverbs 31:30). This is the difference between the transitory and the permanent, between what passes away and what lasts. It confronts us with a choice. We can live for what our culture chases—the things that change from one day to the next. Or we can live for what lasts forever.

A hundred years ago, daily newspapers printed a poem on the first page of each issue. Much of that poetry was second-rate. But a poem titled "The Winds of Fate" by Ella Wheeler

Wilcox caught my attention because the image it used spoke to the choices we make each day of our lives. The opening lines are worth repeating:

> One ship drives east and another drives west
> With the selfsame winds that blow.
>   'Tis the set of the sails
>   And not the gales
> Which tells us the way to go.

It's the set of the sail. Our woman of strength chose to set the sail of her life to live in the presence of the living God. She had a choice, and she chose what lasts forever, disdaining what passes away. In that choice, her life reflected the values of her Maker. In the end, her choice brought her praise, not merely from her family and her community, but from the God before whom she lived. We also have that choice before us. What we choose determines our destination. How are we setting the sail of our life?

The tasks we've been examining in this book are not the point. They are simply the fruit of this *hayil* woman's fear of the Lord. The point of the poem is that when we understand how loved we are by God, our "fear" becomes love in return. We each choose the tasks we believe help us to image God—to reflect His likeness and nature—in our own world. For one woman, imaging God may mean a commitment to nurture each of her children or reach out to neighbors in need of friendship. For another woman, imaging God may mean doubling down in a difficult job at work so she speaks truth in ways others can understand and follow. For still another woman, imaging God may mean pursuing advanced studies in order to implement needed changes in the way we think about medicine or investments or law.

In every case, as we choose how we can image God in our own backyard, we are called to be worthy of trust, diligent in pursuit of imaging God in that environment, and careful how we use our tongue in all we say. These are ways we live out the fear of the Lord. The *hayil* woman in Proverbs 31 gives us the basics for anyone in the home or in business. It's all about how each of us can image God where we live and work. It's true that "charm is deceptive, and beauty is fleeting, but a woman who fears the LORD is to be praised." So whatever else we do, we seek to recognize the difference between what lasts and what passes away. Then we give ourselves to what lasts. Choosing what lasts will be different for each person. At the same time, we pay attention to the praise our *hayil* woman received from her family and from the community: it came because of her choice to fear the Lord. That is the one choice that is common to us all.

Stuart Olyott captured that in these words:

> The fear of God is a habit of mind which acknowledges him at every step, and which views everything in relation to him who is eternally holy, just, and good. It is not the degrading and demoralizing dread of his power such as can be found in many pagan religions, but an inward attitude which loves him, is aware that life is lived in his presence and which longs to please him. It nurses the sincere and heartfelt intention to live for him, not for oneself, but for him![15]

Grab hold of that and its truth will make you strong, a *hayil* person, living your best life possible for God in this broken world.

Lord, it's too easy for me to cower in fear when I think about your greatness. Help me remember that you are love in your very nature, and that you really love me with a love that will not let me go. I feel so unworthy of such love! I need help in living into that love. I pray that with your help, I can truly believe I am loved by God. I know that will change everything for me. Thank you, through Jesus my Savior. Amen.

For Reflection or Discussion

1. When you've thought about God, what were your feelings and reactions?

2. What experiences have you had—positive or negative—with charming people?

3. What criteria do you use to evaluate what is truly beautiful?

4. How do you see "the fear of the Lord" in the light of this chapter?

Notes

1. W. P. Livingstone, *Mary Slessor of Calabar: Pioneer Missionary* (Santa Rosa, CA: Pacific Gates Press, 2016), 33. Originally published in 1880 by Hodder & Stoughton, the book is now available in the public domain.
2. Quoted in Livingstone, 59.
3. Livingstone, 96.
4. While most translators chose rubies as the precious stone mentioned in this text, one translator named the jewels as corals and another as pearls. In the case of highest monetary value, rubies may be the best choice here.
5. Laura M. Holson, "Murders by Intimate Partners Are on the Rise, Study Finds," *New York Times*, April 12, 2019, https:// www.nytimes.com/2019/04/12/us/domestic-violence-victims .html.
6. "January 31, 2018: New England Compounding Center Pharmacist Sentenced for Role in Nationwide Fungal Meningitis Outbreak," Food and Drug Administration, last modified January 31, 2019, https://www.fda.gov/inspections-compliance -enforcement-and-criminal-investigations/press-releases /january-31-2018-new-england-compounding-center-pharmacist -sentenced-role-nationwide-fungal.
7. Thomas P. McCreesh, "Biblical Sound and Sense: Poetic Sound Patterns in Proverbs 10–29," *Journal of Semitic Studies 308*, no. 1 (Spring 1993), 147.
8. From the Old Syriac translation of the Gospels, the prayer actually asks for two things: bread for today and confidence that tomorrow we'll have enough.

9. Quoted by Bruce K. Waltke, *The Book of Proverbs Chapters 15–31* (Grand Rapids: Eerdmans, 2005), 527.

10. Victor H. Matthews, *Manners and Customs in the Bible: An Illustrated Guide to Daily Life in Bible Times* (Peabody, MA: Hendrickson, 1988, 1991), 106.

11. Temper Longman, *Proverbs* (Grand Rapids, MI: Baker Academic, 2006), 546.

12. Bruce K. Waltke, *The Book of Proverbs, Chapters 15–31*, vol. 2, The New International Commentary on the Old Testament (Grand Rapids, MI: William B. Eerdmans, 2005), 513.

13. Shakespeare, *King Lear,* act 5, sc. 3.

14. Alice Mathews, *Gender Roles and the People of God: Rethinking What We Were Taught about Men and Women in the Church* (Grand Rapids: Zondervan, 2017), 165ff.

15. Stuart Olyott, quoted in T. M. Moore *Ecclesiastes: Ancient Wisdom When All Else Fails* (Downers Grove IL: InterVarsity, 2001), 112.